ISBN: 978-0-9894338-7-7
Cover and Art Design: Jenna Stanbrough

Roho Publishing
4040 Graphic Arts Road
Emporia, KS 66801

www.rohopublishing.com

About Roho Publishing

When Kip Keino defeated Jim Ryun in the 1968 Olympic Games at 1500 meters, he credited the win to "Roho." Roho is the Swahili word for spirit demonstrated through extraordinary strength and courage. The type of courage and strength that can be summoned up from deep within that will allow you to meet your goals and overcome the challenges in life. Roho Publishing focuses on the spirit of sport and is designed to inspire, encourage, motivate and teach valuable life lessons.

Dedication

To all the coaches who make track and field fun. Your creative and positive attitude coupled with your passion towards track and field helps create a lifelong commitment for athletes to enjoy physical activity. The enjoyment received by your athletes has created lasting positive memories of track and field as well as offered tremendous positive benefits physically, psychologically, and socially. You make a difference in developing not only the physical components, but also the heart and minds of athletes.

A special dedication to Coach Zach Kindler, whose time on earth was short, but the powerful impact he made on young lives will last forever. Coach Kindler served as a positive role model for both coaches and athletes as a tremendous coach and an even better person.

Acknowledgements

To my family who have supported my passion for the greatest sport in the world—track and field. My wife, Wendy, has supported my endeavors in track and field as an athlete, coach, official and fan.

To my three daughters: Bethany, Leslie, Jenna, who have enjoyed participating in track and field and have remained die-hard track and field fans.

To Jenna, whose talents in developing this book have been invaluable. Her creative talents have been displayed in her artistic work involved in the layout, diagrams, covers and reviews.

To Alaina Fairbanks, for her contributions to the Pole Vault games.

Table of Contents

Index

High Jump Games

Long Jump Games

Triple Jump Games

Pole Vault Games

Jump Games

Shot Put Games

Discus Games

Javelin Games

Hammer Throw Games

Throw Games

Sprint Games

Hurdle Games

Distance Games

Relay Games

Preface

Track and Field Games contains over 200 track and field games (with variations, over 500) that coaches can use to create an enjoyable and productive practice environment. The numerous track and field games help teach the fundamentals and focus on skills required to become a more compete track and field athlete. The games are particularly useful for beginning and intermediate athletes and can be adapted to accommodate more traditional training with experienced athletes. The exercises are designed to challenge athletes and keep them active, motivated and thoroughly involved. The games are competitive and fun to play and they can be easily adapted to different ages and abilities. Both novice and experienced athletes alike will respond favorably to the activities in which they are excited and enthused about. The track and field games provided in this book are designed to create such an enthusiastic and positive attitude.

It is not the intent of this book to give technical advice on "how to perform" the event correctly. Nor is it the intent to supply training programs and plans for athletes. The intent is to supply fun games that have specific objectives to develop athletes. *Track and Field Games* combines fun with skill instruction and practice. The games are designed to utilize different approaches to track and field events while maximizing the development of physical skills.

This book is organized into 11 chapters. Chapters 2-6 focus on the jumping events. Chapters 7-11 focus on the throwing events. Chapters 12-15 focus on the running events, hurdles, and relays. Although categorized by their primary focus, most games emphasize essential elements to many events track and field. An activity that appears in one of the event-specific sections may be able to be used or modified for use in other events as well.

Organization

The games have been organized in an easy to understand format as described below.

Objective: Coaches should consider a game's objectives to determine if the game fits into the specific practice session.

Description: This section supplies the directions in how to set up and run the activity effectively. Group size and field dimensions are provided only as general guidelines and should be adjusted to the ability level of athletes. In some games a scoring system has been provided to add an element of competition to the game. It should be clearly understood that the ultimate aim of each game is for athletes to challenge themselves to achieve a higher standard of performance. Use competitive games only when athletes are ready for competition. Be aware that competitive games may take the focus away from learning (the process) and place it on winning (the product). Many of the games in the book are small-group games, which offer high levels of activity.

Variations: These suggestions provide possible modification and adaptations of the games to offer more variety. The variations also may be used to adjust the difficulty and conditioning involved in the activity. Many of the variations allow the more naturally athletic or competitive athletes to enjoy play, while not exposing the less competitive athlete's weakness.

Equipment: Most activities and games in this book have been designed to use a minimal amount of equipment and are easy to set up. Cones, balls, and ropes are some of the most common equipment items the games call for. If possible, use the maximum amount of equipment to give the athletes more practice time and more fun. Engage the athletes in play instead of waiting in turn.

Safety

Participation in track and field carries an inherent risk of injury, but coaches can minimize the risk by setting up the playing area with safety in mind, giving clear instructions that emphasize safety, and making modifications as needed. Coaches are encouraged to visualize how they want the game to progress and if the game does not conform to expectations, stop the activity and make adjustments.

Chapter 1 - Introduction

Track and field events are among the oldest of all sporting competitions, as running, jumping and throwing are natural and universal forms of human activity. The first recorded examples of organized track and field events occurred in the Ancient Olympic Games held in 776 BC in Olympia, Greece. The only event contested at the first Olympic Games was the "stadion" footrace, a 200-meter race inside the stadium. The events of the Olympic Games expanded to include further running competitions and eventually added field events to evolve into the track and field events we know today.

Track and field events are divided into three major categories: track events, field events, and combined events. Track events involve running on a track over specified distances as well as the hurdling and steeplechase events. There are also relay races in which teams of four athletes run and pass a baton to their team members.

There are two types of field events: jumps, and throws. In jumping competitions, the horizontal jumps consist of the long jump and triple jump and are judged on the length of the jumps, while the vertical jumps consist of the high jump and pole vault and are judged on the height of the jumps. The throwing events involve throwing an implement: shot put, discus, javelin or hammer from a set point, with athletes being judged on the distance that the implement is thrown.

Combined events involve athletes contesting a number of different track and field events. Points are given for their performance in each event and the athlete with the greatest points total at the end of all the events is the winner.

Track and field has remained the second most popular sport in the world behind soccer with millions of athletes participating. Competitions exist for all ages from youth to masters.

Why do athletes participate in sports and specifically, why do athletes participate in track and field? Numerous surveys indicate that young athletes most often list their sport goals in the following order of importance:

- To have fun
- To improve skills and learn new ones
- To be with friends or make new ones
- For thrills and excitement
- To win
- To become physically fit

The findings clearly indicate that the primary goal of many adults of winning is far less important to youth. What really matters to youth is having fun! Striving to win is important, but what's most important is the joy of the activity. The "fun" factor emphasizes the need for positive coaching that goes beyond the focus of winning and losing. Winning is great, and a desired quality to strive for, but not at the expense of fun. There is a strong need for coaches and mentors to guide youth and ingrain positive values and sportsmanship, while also highlighting the importance of education and physical fitness to succeed in life. Coaches with the knowledge and skills necessary to effectively work with track and field athletes can create positive experiences and make a significant difference in the lives of others.

Studies have shown that about 70 percent of kids stop playing organized sports by middle school. They give up participating in sports to pursue other endeavors, many of which are not going to provide the physical activity that youth require to be healthy. Coaches often erroneously feel that learning sport skills is incompatible with fun. Focus and fun are not incompatible; in fact, focus is necessary for fun to occur. Fun is a major motivational factor for continued persistence in any activity.

What can coaches do to ensure that players have fun in practices? Consider the following coaching activities that help to develop the components of fun.

- Match challenges with athletic abilities. Coaches must be sure that the challenges they present to their players are commensurate with their abilities.

- Help athletes focus on the task. Practice sessions should be planned to allow for minimal time of inactivity. When athletes are standing in long lines in coach-directed drills, boredom sets in quickly, and players will seek pleasure by directing attention to things other than the task at hand. Decreasing "down time" increases the athlete's ability to maintain focus.

- Give players a sense of control. Focus games on the athletes, not on the coaches. Set games up for athletes to succeed and athletes will feel they have control over outcomes. It works best to also give players some say in the games and rules they are playing.

- Try to minimize players' self-consciousness. Self-consciousness in athletics is largely fear of what others think of performance. Correcting fear of failure isn't easy, but when athletes can have fun, it's less likely they will feel self-conscious.

Adapting Games

A successful coach adapts an activity to both group and individual needs to insure a more positive activity experience. Each track and field event has its characteristic needs and skills. The following adaptation methods and techniques are outlined as suggestions to ponder when attempting to enhance the learning potential and success of an activity.

Change the space or participation within the playing area
Change the boundaries or the distance
Increase or decrease the number of players
Use equipment that will increase or reduce the range of play
Small group games for more opportunities for activity

Change the time or intensity element
Change the walk to a jog or run transition or vice versa
Increase or reduce time periods for a run or rest

Partner sets where one runs, the other rests, stretches, or performs a physical activity
Add additional repetitions for more activity

Modify the rules
Change the order in relay or team play
Change or add rules in the middle of the activity to "equalize" competition
Add elements of cooperation and problem solving for team bonding
Create exercises for eliminated or waiting players

As coaches plan track and field activities for a session, adaptation must be considered a necessary part of the planning process. Enjoyable appropriate games are a significant vehicle toward enhancing the psychomotor, cognitive, and affective growth of athletes.

Chapter 2 - High Jump

The first recorded high jump event took place in Scotland in the 19th century. Early jumpers used either a straight-on approach or a scissors technique. Through the years, the high jump technique has evolved through the standing high jump, the eastern roll, the western roll, the straddle and finally the flop technique (named after the originator, Dick Fosbury), which is predominately used by jumpers today.

Jumpers must take off on one foot. A jump is considered a foul if the bar is dislodged by the action of the jumper while jumping or the jumper touches the ground or breaks the plane of the near edge of the bar before clearance. Three consecutive missed jumps, at any height or combination of heights, will eliminate the jumper from competition. The jumper who clears the greatest height is the winner.

The ability to convert horizontal velocity to vertical height is a major attribute in high jumping success. Numerous games in the high jump chapter are designed to develop the rhythm of the "J" approach, increase approach speed, and to place the jumper in an advantageous position for take-off. Some of the games focus on the arching during the flight, while, many of the games are designed to work on increasing power that is essential to jumping high.

Safety in the high jump is a priority. The pit should meet national standards with the standards properly set up and secured. The cross bar should always be checked for integrity for signs of cracks. Use of a bungee cord is advised for many games, as it is softer when missed and saves time replacing the crossbar. High jump coaches should always consult their specific rulebook regarding jumping facilities and equipment and follow the important information regarding equipment specifications and safety.

High Jump Obstacle Course

Objective: To integrate jumping rhythm, scissors jumping, and curve running

Description: Set up an obstacle course in a circular pattern with different types of jumps. The jumpers will navigate the course to see who can complete the obstacle course the fastest. If possible, include in the course curve running to simulate the approach, a scissors jump over a low object, a pop-up over a cone, a low hurdle, a horizontal jump (such as jumping over two ropes) and something to jump and reach for.

Variations: (1) Complete the event as a relay. (2) The obstacle course could be run as a team competition with each individual's score added to the team total, low score wins. (3) To reinforce proper technique, points can be awarded for good technical jumps.

15

Equipment: Cones, tape, or line to mark curve, ropes, small cones and crossbar, low hurdles

Weave Relay

Objective: To practice running curved patterns

Description: Form groups of four to six athletes. Set up courses of small cones in a slalom pattern. Each group has its own course to run through. The athletes line up in single file, and the first athlete in line will run the slalom course with the athlete going around the last cone and returning back to the starting line weaving in and out of the cones. Once the first athlete returns to the starting line, he/she touches hands with the second athlete in line, who runs down and back weaving through the cones to touch hands with the third athlete. The relay continues for a certain time period or until everyone has ran through the cones a certain number of times.

Variations: Conduct the event as a shuttle relay race. The first, third and fifth athletes will be at one end and the second, fourth and sixth athletes will be at the other end.

Equipment: Small cones

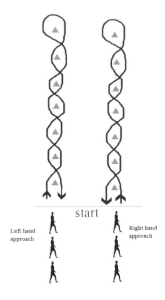

Timed Figure Eight

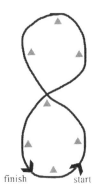

Objective: To develop the ability to run a fast curve approach

Description: Use cones to mark a 20-meter course. Set the cones in a figure eight pattern. The athlete will run a figure eight to complete the course. Emphasize the athlete running tall and leaning into the curve. Time each athlete to see how fast he or she can run the figure eight course.

Variations: (1) Run the course relay style. (2) Run at least three times and see if athletes can improve their time.

Equipment: Cones, stopwatch, recording sheet

16

Circle Gears

Objective: To develop the rhythm and speed on a curve approach

Description: Set up an inner circle 10 meters in diameter with small cones. Jumpers who approach from the right side will run a counter-clockwise circle around the inside circle of cones. Set up an outer circle 12 meters in diameter with small cones. Jumpers who approach from the left side will run a clockwise circle in the outer circle. Jumpers will stand at least three feet from each other to start. The first athlete in one of the lines will be the leader designated to make gear change calls. The speeds will be on a scale of 1-5, with 1st gear being slow and 5th being very fast. On a signal, the leader yells "1" and the jumpers start to run their circle in gear "1." Jumpers should lean in to the curve on the run so the body weight is on the inside of the curve. After a lap, the leader will yell "2," which is the signal to pick it up. After one more lap, the jumpers run a "3" speed for a lap and follow that with one lap at a "4" speed. The last speed is a "5" speed for the last lap. Athletes should stay in line order and are not allowed to pass anyone in their line.

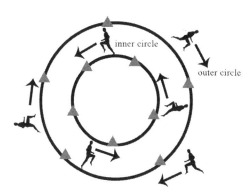

Recover for a designated time period and repeat with the athletes alternating the use of the inner circle. Continue for a designated number of rounds.

Variations: (1) Jumpers are allowed to pass other runners while running the circle. (2) Time individually to see who can run the fastest circle for the last lap. (3) Extend the five gears to three laps. (4) Alternate back and forth between gears (i.e., three to two to four to three to five). (5) The gear speeds are randomly called out.

Equipment: Cones, stopwatch

Circle Run-Simon Says

Objectives: To practice running the high jump curve

Description: Set up an inner circle 10 meters in diameter with small cones. Jumpers who approach from the right side, will run a counter-clockwise circle around the inside circle of cones. Set up an outer circle 12 meters in diameter with small cones. Jumpers who approach from the left side will run a clockwise circle in the outer circle. Jumpers will stand at least three feet from each other to start. On a signal, the jumpers start to run their circle. After 30 seconds, the leader indicates an activity by saying "Simon says do bounding." All the jumpers will continue around the circle bounding. After 15-30 seconds, the leader will change the activity by saying something similar to "Simon says take three steps and pop-up." Athletes continue to run the curve and perform called out activities. However, if the leader does not say "Simon says" then athletes should continue the previous activity. Any athlete changing the activity when

"Simon" did not say to, must exit to the inside of the circle and jog in a clockwise direction until "Simon says" to do another activity and then the athlete may re-enter the game. Periodically change "Simon" and have the right hand approach jumpers switch to the outer circle (still running counterclockwise) and the left hand approach jumpers move to the inner circle (still running clockwise).

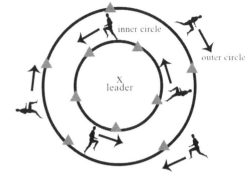

Variations: Here are some recommended activities to do on the circle: (1) bounding, (2) change direction, (3) speed up, (4) high knees, (5) three steps and pop-up, (6) left leg jumping, (7) right leg jumping, (8) hopping on both feet. (9) Change or add your own.

Equipment: Cones to form circles

1 Step, 2 Step, 3 Step, 4

 Objective: To practice take-offs from short approaches

Description: Jumpers line up to jump and take a one-step approach, jumping with the bar at a low height. Each jumper is allowed three misses at a height before they are out. If the jumper clears the height, he/she remains in the competition and will continue to compete in the one-step jump as the bar continues to go up. Continue to raise the bar until the final jumper is out. Record the final mark (in inches or centimeters) the jumpers clear before going out. When all the jumpers are out at the one-step height, move to the two-step approach. Complete the same procedure as the one-step approach, until a winner is determined and record the height cleared at the two-step approach. Move to the three-step jump and then the four-step approach. When the four-step approach competition is completed, the jumper with the most total number of inches (or centimeters) cleared is the winner.

Variations: (1) Form teams and add the scores of each individual to obtain a team score. (2) Continue jumping from more than a four-step approach.

Equipment: High jump set-up (pit, standards, crossbar), recording sheet

Time The J

Objective: To practice approach speed

Description: Jumpers line up in single file line. The jumpers will run their full approach one at a time. The goal is to increase speed with each step of the approach and run 20 meters past the take-off spot. The athlete is timed from the first movement to the 20-meter spot.

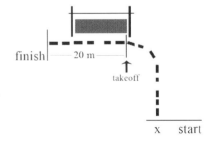

18

Variations: (1) Repeat with the athletes trying to beat their time. (2) Run three trials and take the best score. Emphasize that athletes try to beat their previous time on each trial.

Equipment: High Jump set-up (pit, standards and crossbar), stopwatch, recording sheet

Jump and Reach

Objective: To test vertical jump

Description: Form two teams. On a wall or using a vertical tester, measure the standing height from the end of the fingertip when the athlete is reaching as high as he/she can with both feet entirely on the ground. Then measure the maximal standing vertical jump by having them touch the wall or on a vertical tester. Determine the difference between the standing reach and maximal vertical jump to come up with the vertical jump for each athlete. Take the best of three trials on the maximal vertical jump. Add up the vertical jumps for everyone in a group and get a team total.

Variations: Use as an individual competition.

Equipment: Jump and reach assessment equipment

Pop Weave

Objective: To practice running curved patterns and the take-off

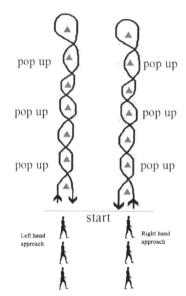

Description: Form groups of four to six athletes. Set up courses of small cones in a slalom pattern. Each group has its own course to run through. The athletes line up in single file. The first athlete in line will run the slalom course weaving in and out of the cones. When the jumper passes near the cones, he/she must simulate the high jump plant by laying back in a plant position and performing a pop-up in the air. The athlete will do a pop-up in the air on every other cone. This allows the athlete to jump on the same curve as his/her take-off approach. When the last cone is reached, the athlete goes around the last cone and returns weaving in and out of the cones doing pop-ups. Once the first athlete returns to the starting line, he/she touches hands with the second athlete in line, who runs down and back weaving through the cones and performing pop-ups at every other cone. The relay continues for a certain time period or until everyone has ran through the cones a certain number of times.

Variations: (1) Challenge the athlete to jump as high as the cone height. (2) Place different height cones for athletes to jump over.

Equipment: Small cones

Use Your Head

Objective: To focus on jumping vertically

Description: From a goal post, hang a tennis ball on a rope from one to two feet above a jumper's head. Start at a height that the athlete will be able to reach and be successful. The ball should hang far enough down that it is at the proper height to hit with the head when jumping properly. Allow the jumpers to get a running start of three to four strides and jump off their take-off foot and attempt to touch the ball with their head. The focus should be a on a proper take-off position and jumping straight up.

Variations: (1) Start with a one-step approach and gradually increase the number of steps. (2) Place a zone from which the athlete must take off and land. Start with a two-foot zone. This forces the athlete to go vertical instead of horizontal. (3) Drop the ball to a lower height and the jumper will touch the ball with his/her inside knee. (4) Hang the ball higher and the jumpers will touch the ball with an extended reach of the hand.

Equipment: Goal posts, rope, tennis ball (you can use Velcro on the rope and tennis ball). Another option is to set up the pole vault standards with a crossbar and hang the ball from the bar.

Shoe Kick

Objective: To take off using a scissors kick

Description: Jumpers untie and loosen the shoe on s inside leg. The jumper will take a short approach to the bar (two to three steps) on the curve, plant their take-off foot and perform a scissors kick. As the jumper drives his/her inside leg up forcefully and powerfully, the jumper attempts to kick their shoe off their foot as far as they can. To complete the scissors kick, the jumper will land with both feet on the pit.

Variations: (1) This can be done without a pit. The jumpers will use a marked line to scissors over and land on their feet. (2) Measure how far the shoe can be kicked. (3) Have a contest to see how high the shoe can be kicked.

Equipment: High Jump set-up (pit, standards and crossbar)

Limbo Lower Now!

Objective: To increase back flexibility for the high jump

Description: Place the standards and crossbar away from the high jump pit so a game of limbo under the high jump bar may be played. For the starting height, set the bar height so all participants can be successful. Athletes line up and go one at a time using correct limbo technique. When the standards will not go any lower, athletes will take turns holding the bar to make it lower. Athletes must go under the bar by walking on their feet keeping the back arched. Athletes are out when they fail to achieve a height.

Variations: Athletes get three attempts at a height before they are out.

Equipment: High jump standards, crossbar

Flip Together

Objective: To work on arch over the bar

Description: Divide into groups of three with everyone in the group of equal ability. The first group will start standing with its athletes' backs against the bar and pit, and using their legs, drive up and backwards over the bar into the pit. All three athletes will jump at the same time with the goal being to synchronize the movements all together. The focus should be on developing a good arch in the back. The coach or fellow group members will judge the jumpers on a scale of 1-10, with 1 being low and 10 being high. The scoring criteria is based on good form while arching, synchronization of the jumpers and clearance. Jumpers should communicate to begin their jumps at the same time. There is synchronized diving in the Olympics, someday there may be synchronized high jump back flipping!

Note: Emphasize all three jumpers to spread out along the bar for safety purposes.

Variations: (1) Start off without the bar. (2) Use a bungee cord in place of the cross bar. (3) Conduct a team competition to see which team can go the highest. A clearance is all three team members clearing the bar. A team gets three misses at a height before they are out.

Equipment: High jump set-up (pit, standards, cross bars) bungee cord

Pick Under Pressure

Objective: To take jumps under pressure

Description: Form two teams of equal abilities. Each jumper will select three heights to jump at and will receive one jump at each of their selected heights. Each increasing height will score higher for the team. If the jumper clears the height, the number of inches (or centimeters) cleared are counted as points for the team. If the jumper does not clear the height, zero points are received. The team with the most points after everyone has completed their three jumps is declared the winner. Jumpers can decide whether they want to risk taking a chance for high points they may possibly miss or take jumps at lower heights where the odds of clearance are higher.

Variations: (1) This can be conducted as an individual competition. (2) The heights can be set by the coach so that everyone has a chance to be successful at one of the heights.

Equipment: High jump set-up (pit, standards, crossbar), recording sheet

Jump the Great Height

Objective: To practice jumping high heights in a team environment

Description: Form two groups of equal abilities. Each team will predict how many jumps it will take to clear the heights of people, monuments, etc. that they select. All made jumps are recorded to see how close the athletes are to their predictions. Each jumper in every group gets a chance to jump at least one height. Here are some examples:

Great Wall of China
Height of basketball goal
Height of Michael Jordan
World record in men's high jump
World record in women's high jump

Variations: (1) All teams compete at the same selected goal to see which team can achieve it first. (2) Select higher goal heights, allowing the jumpers to take multiple jumps to reach the height.

Equipment: High jump set-up (pit, standards, crossbar), recording sheet

Go Bananas HJ

 Objectives: To keep athletes focused and involved in a jumping activity as they wait in line to jump

Description: Athletes line up to high jump at heights designated by the coach. The first jumper in line approaches the bar and jumps. If the jumper clears the bar, everyone in line jumps vertically as high as they can in place one time. Periodically, after a jumper clears the bar, the coach will yell "Go Bananas!" and everyone will jump as high as they can (in place) for three consecutive jumps.

Variations: (1) After a clearance by a jumper, the first jumper in line does one jump, the second jumper in line does two jumps, the third jumper in line does three jumps, continuing down the line to the last person, with each person performing the number of jumps associated with the position in line. (2) After a clearance, everyone in line does one vertical jump. After two consecutive clearances by jumpers in the line, everyone does two jumps to celebrate the clearance. After a third consecutive clearance by the line, the line does three jumps. Continue to perform the number of jumps associated with the number of consecutive clearances. When the line has a miss, the count will start over.

Equipment: High jump set-up (pit, standards, crossbar)

J-U-M-P

Objective: To jump under the pressure of trying to match other jumpers

Description: This game is similar to H-O-R-S-E in basketball. Divide into groups of three to four jumpers. The personal record for each jumper is recorded (PR). Within the group, Jumper 1 is up first and states what he/she will attempt to achieve. For example, Jumper 1 states he/she will clear one foot below his/her PR on a five-step approach. Jumper 1 attempts the bar at one foot below the PR with a five-step approach. If Jumper 1 achieves it, the rest of the jumpers have to attempt the bar at one foot below their PR on a five-step approach. If a jumper misses, a letter is given; the first letter is J. On subsequent misses, the athlete will receive the rest of the letters, U-M-P. If the athlete misses at the final letter—P—he/she receives a second final attempt. If the jumper misses the second final attempt, JUMP has been spelled and the athlete is out of the game. If Jumper 1 does not clear the bar on the first attempt, then the next jumper does not have to match it and Jumper 2 will state what he/she will achieve. If Jumper 2 clears, then the rest of the group must match it or get a letter. Continue until one jumper remains.

Variations: (1) Make sure the groups are fairly equal in talent and use the same height for everyone. (2) Once a person is eliminated, he/she performs high jump drills. (3) While one group is competing in the game, the other groups will do drills or other high jump games.

Examples of attempts to be taken:
Clear bar one foot below PR on full step scissors approach.
Clear bar 16 inches below PR on standing back flip over bar.

Equipment: High jump set-up (pit, standards, crossbar)

High Jump Tournament

Objective: To jump in head-to-head competition in a fun but challenging environment

Description: Divide into groups of four to eight jumpers of equal ability. If there are three jumpers in a four-jumper bracket, one will receive a bye. If there are five jumpers in the eight-jumper bracket, there will be three byes. Each jumper will draw a number to determine his/her draw in the tournament. Two jumpers in the bracket will jump against each other. Each jumper has three jumps at each height. The winner of the bracket is the jumper who clears the most number of times in the three jumps. If they are tied, use a tiebreaker of one more jump at that height. If both jumpers make the bar, raise it two inches. The jumper that takes the height advances in the tournament. If the jumpers do not break the tie at that height, play rock-paper-scissors. The winner of the bracket moves onto the next round. Start the bar at eight inches below the jumper's PR.

Note: Jumpers may be competing against each other head-to-head but both be jumping at different heights (based upon their PRs). The height setting for the second round is based upon how the jumper performed on the previous round.

If jumper cleared all 3 jumps at the height- raise 2"
If jumper cleared 2 jumps at height- raise 1"
If jumper clearcd 1 jump- keep at same height
If jumper missed all three- lower 2"

Variations: (1) Conduct the tournament jumping head-to-head (not based on PR). To allow all jumpers to receive the same number of jumps, run a consolation side of the bracket.

Equipment: High Jump set up (pit, standards, cross bar), tournament recording sheet

5-8 person bracket

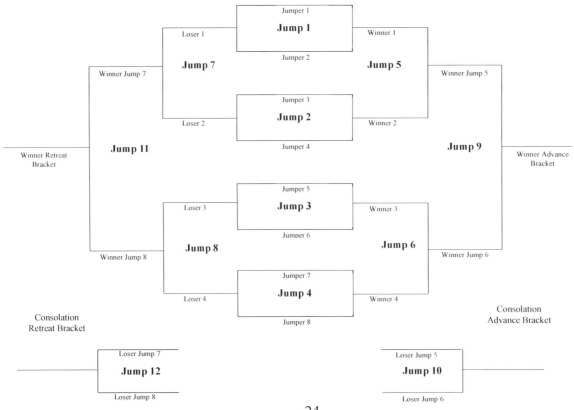

24

1-4 person bracket

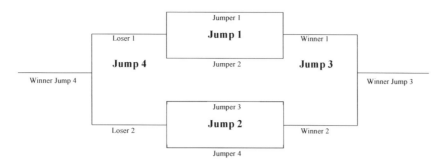

Climbing the Ladder

Objective: To jump under pressure

Description: Divide into groups of three to five jumpers. The better jumpers should be spread evenly throughout the groups. Each group is given ten total attempts with every jumper having to jump at least two times. The jumpers can determine the height of the bars they will jump at. Every time a bar is cleared that distance (in inches or centimeters) is added to the team's height. A missed bar would be a zero, but will count as one of the ten attempts. The team with the highest cumulative height will be the winner.

Variations: Make the last attempt a bonus attempt. If cleared the team gets four more inches or 10 centimeters in bonus points.

Equipment: High jump set-up (pit, standards, cross bar), recording sheet

Jump That Bar

Objective: To jump under pressure of a challenge

Description: Divide into groups where everyone has a partner of equal ability. The first person in the group makes a bid in the form of an original challenge statement to his/her group. An example would be jumper 1 says, "I can make that jump in five steps." Jumper 2 can say, "make that jump" meaning Jumper 1 won the bid. If Jumper 1 makes the jump, Jumper 1 gets one point. If Jumper 1 misses the jump, Jumper 2 gets one point. However, Jumper 2 can accept the original challenge and better it by saying "I can make that jump in four steps." Jumper 2 would win the bid and jump at four steps and if a clearance is made, receives a point, and if missed, Jumper 1 gets the point.

Variations: (1) Continue the bidding if Jumper 2 accepts the challenge, Jumper 1 can up the bid. Examples of challenges: (2) standing back flip, (3) number of steps to scissors bar at certain height, (4) number of steps on approach, (5) height off regular approach.

Equipment: High jump set-up (pit, standards, crossbar)

Team Tic-Tac-Toe

Objective: To jump from a short approach in a fun game

Description: Form two teams with one team the X's and the other team as the O's. Start at a height that the lowest jumper can clear. Each team will take turns alternating jumps. If a jumper makes the height, he/she will get to place the mark for the team on the tic-tac-toe recording sheet. If a jumper does not make the height, no mark may be placed. Continue to play until one team wins. Start another game and continue until you reach the number of desired jumps.

Variations: (1) Form teams of just two people and make it an individual challenge. (2) Form small groups of three to five people of equal ability.

Equipment: High jump set-up (pit, standards, crossbar), recording sheet

Chapter 3 - Long Jump

The long jump is one of the most natural events in track and field. Like all early track events, it was a form of training for warfare of crossing streams and ravines. The long jump uses a runway, a takeoff board, and a sand pit. The objective is for the athlete to jump as far forward as possible.

Many of the jumping games in this book have been designed for use with or without a sand pit. The standing long jump is used as a beginning phase and activities progress to full approaches. Often in the early stages of learning, it is helpful to develop the approach on the track rather than on the runway to eliminate the distraction of the board and pit. Attaining a high velocity is important to success in the jump but speed should not be developed at the expense of incorrect mechanics. Many of the games involve developing the proper step approach and the take-off. Other games focus on the flight and landing, and several games help develop the power needed to become a successful jumper.

Safety should be always be a high priority. Sand pits should be free of debris and regularly spaded to keep the sand loose. The pit should be watered periodically to keep the sand slightly moist. The boards should be level with the runway and not protrude above the runway or surrounding ground. The take-off board should be visible, stable, and located at a reasonable distance from the sand pit. The sand should be kept at the level of the board and runway. Keep the area behind the pit open so athletes may run through safely. The area around the pit, including behind it, should be free of all obstructions. Long jump coaches should always consult their specific rulebook regarding jumping facilities and equipment and follow the important information regarding equipment specifications and safety.

River Leap

Objective: To develop dynamic coordination and rhythm

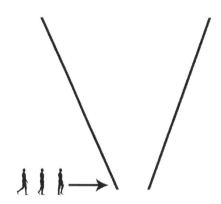

Description: Stretch out two ropes on the ground. Use the ropes to form a single large "V". The space between the two ropes is the river. Athletes take turns running and leaping over the river. Athletes should start leaping at the narrow part of the river and progress to leaping wider parts. With beginning athletes, focus on the take-off with one foot and landing with two feet while bending the knees.

Variations: (1) Conduct the river leap as a relay. (2) Pretend there are crocodiles in the river and one must clear the gators!

Equipment: Open outdoor space with soft grass, two long ropes

Steps

Objectives: To develop consistency in the long jump approach

Description: Jumpers will take full approaches focusing on proper acceleration. The edge of the long jump board closest to the pit will be the zero line. Record to the closest inch or centimeter how far a jumper's toe is off from the end of the board (zero line). A jumper can be short of the board or over the board. For example, if the jumper is three inches short of the edge of the board with his/her toe, he/she will receive a three. If the jumper is four inches over the board, he/she receives a score of four. Take a number of approaches and add up the scores. Low score wins. Emphasize jumpers to run through the board.

Variations: (1) The game can be played on or off a runway. (2) Conduct in a team competition.

Equipment: Long jump set-up (pit, rake), tape measure, recording sheet

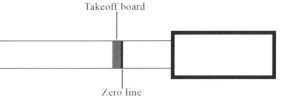

On Board

Objective: To practice consistency on the approach

Description: Develop a take-off area of a 4-inch (10 cm) front area, a 16-inch (40 cm) center area, and a 4-inch (10 cm) back area. Each jumper will take a full approach run-through. Emphasize jumpers to run through the board.
Scores are recorded as following.

If the center area is achieved = 3 points
1 point for hitting the front or back areas
0 point = missing the takeoff area
The jumper with the most points after a designated number of run-throughs wins the game.

Variations: (1) The game can be played on or off a runway. (2) Form teams with the total for each individual used.

Equipment: Long jump set-up (pit, rake), tape measure, cones or marking material, recording sheet

Jump for Distance

Objective: To develop the take-off phase

Description: Designate a take-off zone from one foot in front of the board to one foot behind the board on the runway. This will be wider than a typical board but allows the jumper to focus more on jumping than trying to hit the board. Mark the take-off area with cones, tape or chalk. Place hula hoops in the long jump pit in a line with the first hoop closest to the take-off area. Continue to place the hoops down at a distance that is equal to the best jumper's ability. Hoop one is equal to one point; hoop two equals two points, and so on.

Divide into two different teams. Each jumper will take a short approach (two to four steps) to the take-off area and jump and land in a hula hoop. Record the results for each athlete. The better of three trials is scored for the total of the team. The sum of the individual bests will be added to tally the team total. No points are awarded if the jumper does not land at least one foot in a hoop.

Variations: (1) Conduct the event as an individual competition. (2) The athlete scores two points if both feet land in the hoop. (3) Extend the number of steps taken by the athlete on the approach.

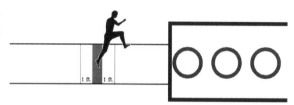

Equipment: Long jump set-up (pit, rake), hula hoops, cones, tape, or chalk, recording sheet

Long Jump 1 Step, 2 Step, 3 Step, 4

Objective: To practice short approaches

Description: Each jumper takes a jump off a one-step approach. The distance is recorded. Each jumper then takes a jump off a two-step approach with the distance recorded. Continue with a three-step approach, followed by a four-step approach and jump. Add up the distance for each jumper. The jumper with the farthest distance is declared the winner.

Variations: (1) Measure from where a jumper actually takes off instead of the take-off board. (2) Continue jumping more than 4 jumps. (3) Conduct as a team event. (4). Allow jumpers multiple attempts at each approach length.

Equipment: Long jump set-up (pit, rakes), recording sheet

Mound Jump

Objective: To keep feet high in the air during the long jump flight

Description: Build up a mound of sand in the long jumping pit two feet less than the athlete can jump in the standing long jump. Athletes will take a standing jump attempting to clear the mound of sand. Athletes will focus on keeping their legs up to avoid hitting the sand mound. The legs should be extended for the landing. When the athlete is successful, the mound of sand should be extended so it becomes progressively more difficult to clear. This activity will help the jumpers to keep their feet up in mid-air during the flight.

Variations: (1) Gradually add running steps to the approach. (2) Continue moving the mound of sand farther and farther into the pit.

Equipment: Long jump set-up (pit, rakes)

Hitch Kick

Objective: To learn the concept of the hitch kick

Description: Place a two-foot high cross bar on cones in the long jump pit about six feet away from the take-off spot. The athlete will take a three-to five-step approach, jump over the cross bar and try to the knock the crossbar off the cones on the backward motion of the legs. Athletes bring the take-off leg forward, the legs scissor in the air as they attempt to claw the cross bar with the foot of leading leg. The athlete will land in a kneeling position with the take-off leg ahead. Eventually, the athlete will be able to kick and land with both legs together. This activity simulates the action of the hitch kick jump.

Variations: (1) Move the cross bar further into the pit, but at a distance the athlete can clear. (2) Increase the length of the approach.

Equipment: Long jump set-up (pit, rakes), cones, cross bar (a pool noodle or cones work well as a cross bar for beginners)

Team Standing Long Jump

Objective: To develop power by performing a standing long jump

Description: Form two or more equal teams. Each team member will perform a standing long jump. Add each team member's jump to obtain a cumulative distance.

Variations: (1) Perform three long jumps for each athlete and add up for a cumulative distance. (2) Perform the activity as an individual event.

Equipment: Long jump set-up (pit, rakes), tape measure, recording sheet

Bounding Long Jump

Objectives: To develop power and rhythm in the take-off

Description: Designate a take-off zone from one foot in front of the board to one foot behind the board on the runway. The athlete will take long "bounding" strides, focusing on swinging the arms up and forward at every stride down the runway. The athlete will take off on one foot when in the take-off zone and jump as far as possible, landing on both feet.

Variations: (1) Alternate taking off between the strong and the weak leg, (2) Perform the activity off the runway

Equipment: Long jump set-up (pit, rake)

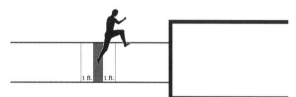

How Far Can You Long Jump?

Objective: To have fun practicing long jump drills to see how far one can go in each drill

Description: Athletes will compete in three different long jumps and tally the total of all three. The first jump the athlete will perform is a standing long jump from the edge of the pit into the sand. The measurement will be taken from where the athlete takes off (toe of front foot) to where the athlete lands. The second jump the athlete will take a two-step approach and jump from the runway. The measurement will be taken from where the athlete takes off (toe of front foot) to where the athlete lands. In the third jump, the athletes will perform a running long jump, starting at their mark and jumping as far as possible into the pit. The measurement will be taken from where the athlete takes off (toe of front foot) to where the athlete lands. After each athlete has gotten a mark for all three jumps, the athlete will add up all three of the jumps. Note the emphasis is on jumping and the measurement is taken from where the athlete takes off, not the long jump board.

Variations: (1) Athletes will compete on teams and add up the individual scores for a team total.

Equipment: Long jump set-up (pit, rakes) tape measure, recording sheet

Ancient Long Jump

Objective: To experience a historical long jumping method

Description: In ancient times a long jumper carried a weight in each hand. He would swing these weights as he ran down the runway and as he jumped he would bring the weights forward to help throw him into the landing pit. This was designed to increase the distance of the jump. The athlete places a two-pound weight in each hand and practices taking short approach jumps into the pit and bringing the weights forwards during the jump. The athlete remains holding on to the weights at all times. Ask the athletes to compare the weighted jumps to the regular jumps. Do they feel the weights gave them an advantage? Note that it is now illegal in track and field to carry the weights.

Variations: (1) Take a short approach (two to four steps) with the weights and measure the distance. Then, take a short approach without the weights and measure the distance. Was there any difference between the lengths of the jumps? (2) Take multiple jumps both ways and measure the difference.

Equipment: Long jump set-up (pits, rake), tape measure, recording sheets, and small weights to hold in hands

One Leg Tag

Objectives: To develop power and rhythm in the jumping leg

Description: Set up a playing area. Two jumpers are designated as taggers. Once a jumper is tagged, he/she becomes a tagger. All jumpers must jump on one leg in the game of tag. The coach or someone designated as a leader calls a command to designate the jumping leg. The taggers and non-taggers all have to jump on one leg. This is a great warm-up game for long jumpers.

Variations: Use a variety of jumping activities involving: (1) bounding, (2) two foot hopping, (3) backwards jumping.

Equipment: Cones to designate the playing area

Frog Tag

Objectives: To develop power and rhythm in the legs

Description: This game is similar to one leg tag. Set up a playing area. Two athletes are designated as taggers. Everyone can run around within the playing area, but once tagged, the athlete must get down like a frog and jump 3 times saying "ribbit" each time. Play for a designated time and then switch taggers. This is a great warm-up game for long jumpers.

Variations: (1) Once the athlete is tagged and completes the frog jumps, that athlete becomes the tagger. (2) Once the athlete is tagged and completes the frog jumps, that athlete joins the taggers.

Equipment: Cones to mark the playing area

Frog Team

Objective: To develop power in the jumping legs

Description: Form groups of approximately four athletes in single file line. From a starting line the athletes will perform a "frog-jump," a two-foot forward hop. The first jumper in line stands with the tips of the toes at the starting line and jumps forward as far as possible, landing on both feet and keeping the feet planted. The landing point becomes the starting line for the second jumper of the team. The second jumper will stand beside the first jumper and place his/her toes even with the first jumper's heel. The second jumper will then carry out a "frog-jump". The third athlete jumps from the landing point of the second one, and so on. The event is completed when the last member of the team has jumped and that landing point is marked. The team that jumps the farthest is the winner.

Variations: (1) The entire procedure is repeated a second time (second trial). The team scoring is based on the best result of two trials. (2) Jump for a designated time period with the team that has jumped the farthest the winner. (3) Jump with a partner, alternating jumps.

Equipment: None needed

Jump, Throw, Run

Objective: To improve jumping rhythm and coordination

Description: Form two to four teams of equal size. Designate a playing area with a square and a hula hoop in the middle. In the hula hoop place 15-20 balls of different sizes. The groups will line up single file with each group in a corner. Each group will have a hula hoop by its starting line. On command, the first athlete in line jumps on one leg to the middle of the hoop, selects one ball and throws it back to the next teammate in line, who catches it and places it in the hula hoop. If that teammate does not catch it, he/she is the only one able to retrieve it. The athlete then runs back and tags the next teammate. The next teammate will start jumping to the middle and repeat the process. Teams collect as many balls as possible in a time period. When all the balls have been removed from the center the

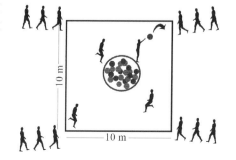

game is over. The goal is to collect the most balls possible.

Variations: (1) The athlete alternates jumping legs on every other turn. (2) Use different objects to jump over. (3) The teammate in line that receives the throw, jumps with the ball and replaces it in the circle.

Equipment: 15-20 balls of different size, cones to mark the playing area, hula hoops

Chapter 4 - Triple Jump

The triple jump is often referred to as the hop, step, and jump. It is similar to the long jump, but the athlete performs a hop, a step and then a jump into the sand pit. The triple jump has its origins in the Ancient Olympics and has been a modern Olympics event since the Games' inception in 1896.

The athlete sprints down a runway to a take-off board, from which the triple jump is measured. The games in this chapter address the hop, step, and jump phases of the triple jump and are designed to develop skills and have fun. A major focus in many of the games is to develop the rhythm and coordination used in the three phases of the hop, step, and jump. These three phases are executed in one continuous sequence. Power, coordination and rhythm need to be developed for athletes to become more proficient in the triple jump.

Safety should be always be a high priority. Sand pits should be free of debris and regularly spaded to keep the sand loose. The pit should be watered periodically to keep the sand slightly moist. The boards should be level with the runway and not protrude above the runway or surrounding ground. The take-off board should be visible, stable, and located at a reasonable distance from the sand pit. The sand should be kept at the level of the board and runway. Keep the area behind the pit open so athletes may run through safely. The area around the pit, including behind it, should be free of all obstructions. Triple jump coaches should always consult their specific rule book regarding jumping facilities and equipment and follow the important information regarding equipment specifications and safety.

Triple Jump Skip

Objective: To develop the triple jump rhythm

Description: Two athletes hold the ends of a skipping rope as the rope turns. The other athletes form a single file line 15 meters behind the rope. On command, the athletes with the rope begin turning the rope while the other athletes hop, bound and jump towards the rope. The goal is to make it over/under the rope without disturbing the rhythm. Reinforce the importance of even rhythm and maintaining speed throughout the jump. Continue for a designated number of times and then rotate rope turners.

Variations: Use other jumping activities such as (1) bounding, (2) right leg hop, (3) left leg hop, (4) skip, and (5) two-foot hop. (6) Use as an individual activity with each athlete turning his/her own rope.

Equipment: Long jump rope to be used for skipping

Triple Jump Hopscotch

Objectives: To develop dynamic balance, coordination, and rhythm required for the triple jump

Description: Draw a hopscotch grid with 10 numbered boxes. Line up in front of the hopscotch grid. The first jumper in line tosses a marker onto square 1. The jumper hops over square 1 and hops through all the other squares on one foot. At the end of the grid, the jumper turns around and jumps all the way back on one foot, pausing to pick up the marker from square 1 and finishes jumping back to the start. The jumper then throws the marker into square 2 and goes again. The jumper continues to repeat until he/she has done the hopscotch grid with the marker in every square. When there are two free squares side by side, the jumper lands one foot in each square at the same time before continuing on one foot.

RULE: If a player steps into the square with the marker, touches any lines, or touches the ground with any body part other than the one foot, that player starts again at square 1.

Variations: (1) Conduct as a relay, so that when the first jumper goes through the jumping grid, the second jumper will start and hop over square 2. Try different hopping actions to go through the course: (2) left foot, (3) right foot, (4) alternate feet, (5) feet together, (6) hopping backwards.

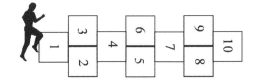

Equipment: Make your own hopscotch grid with chalk

Jump Even

Objective: To practice the rhythm of the triple jump phases

Description: Using ropes or cones, lay out a grid of three lines that get gradually farther apart from each other at one end. Within each grid is the phase landing area. At one end the three lines are close together, at the other end they are the furthest apart. The three lines at any one time should be equidistant to aid in making the three phases of the jump the same length. Athletes start on the narrow end and try to jump in the phase areas using the triple jump sequence. For a greater challenge, continue moving down the grid where the landing phase areas are wider.

Variations: (1) Athletes can clap the rhythm that they hear from the three phases. There should be no variation in time between phases. They could also chant "hop, step, jump" on each phase. (2) Score one point for each time the athlete lands in the proper phase landing area.

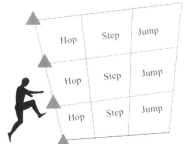

Equipment: Tape measure, rope or cones to mark grids

Triple Jump Rhythm

Objective: To practice the even rhythm of the triple jump phases

Description: Lay out a grid of three lanes consisting of three hula hoops laid end-to-end. In lane one, the three hoops are closer together, in lane two the hoops become further apart and in lane three, the hoops are the furthest apart. One point is scored for every hoop the athlete correctly jumps into. The athlete starts in lane one, takes a run-up of five meters or less, and completes a hop, step, and jump. After completing lane one, the athlete moves into lane two, and then lane three. The score is recorded after every trial with the goal being to score the most points possible. Adjust the hoops based upon the ability level of the athlete.

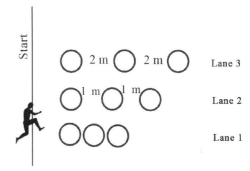

Variations: (1) Add a bonus point if all three grids are correctly hit. (2) Compete in a team competition. Cones could be substituted to jump over to replace the hoops.

Equipment: Tape measure, hula hoops, cones, recording sheet

How Far Can You Triple Jump?

Objective: To have fun practicing the triple jump to see how far one can go

Description: Athletes will compete in three different triple jumps and tally the total of all three. The first jump the athlete will perform is a standing triple jump from the edge of the pit into the sand. The measurement will be taken from where the athlete takes off (toe of front foot) to where the athlete lands. The second triple jump the athlete will take is a two-step approach and jump from the runway. The measurement will be taken from where the athlete takes off (toe of front foot) to where the athlete lands. In the third jump the athletes will perform a running triple jump, starting at their approach mark and jumping as far as they can into the pit. The measurement will be taken from where the athlete takes off (toe of front foot) to where the athlete lands. After each athlete has gotten a mark for all three jumps, they will add up all three of their jumps. Note the emphasis is on jumping and the measurement is taken from where the athlete takes off, not the triple jump board.

Variations: (1) Athletes will compete on teams and add up the individual scores for a team total.

Equipment: Triple jump set-up (pit, rakes) tape measure

37

Leaps and Bounds

Objective: To have fun practicing bounding drills

Description: Mark out a 10-meter zone and a 30-meter zone. Athletes will have three sets of bounding drills they complete for time.

- alternate single leg bounding for 30 meters
- alternate speed bounding for 30 meters
- double leg bounding for 10 meters

Record the times after each bounding exercise. Add up the three bounding drill times for a cumulative time.

Variations: (1) Conduct as a team competition, adding up the individual time for a team total. (2) Increase or decrease the bounding distance. Try the following variations: (3) bound and sprint, (4) hurdle bounding.

Equipment: Cones, hurdles, stopwatch, recording sheet

Find Your Partner

Objective: To develop power and strength in the legs

Description: Mark a playing area boundary. Players move around within the playing area by triple jumping. When a whistle is blown, each athlete must continue triple jumping and jump to find a partner. If one person does not find a partner, that person must do five vertical jumps. Allow the athletes to jog for recovery and when the whistle is blown again, athletes start triple jumping around the area again.

Variations: (1) Vary forming groups of three, four, or five partners. (2) When the whistle is blown once, find one partner, when it is blown twice, find two partners, when blown three times, find three partners. Find the number of partners based upon the number of whistle blasts.

Equipment: Cones to mark the playing area, whistle

Traffic Light Hop-Stop

Objective: Develop power and rhythm in a jumping game

Description: This is a modified version of the old red light/green light game. One athlete will be the leader and will stand on the goal line facing the opposite direction away from the rest of the runners. The leader yells, "hop" and starts clapping. When the leader is clapping, everyone can triple jump. The leader will clap five times, yell, "stop" and then turn around. The jumpers will time their jumping to stop on the fifth clap. If the leader catches anybody jumping after the fifth clap, they must return to the starting line (by running) to start over. The leader turns around facing the opposite direction and yells "hop" and starts clapping again. The jumpers can start jumping again when the leader is clapping. Before the leader starts clapping, the leader can turn around and catch someone if they are jumping. Once the leader starts clapping, five claps must be completed before the leader yells, "stop" and turns around. The first jumper to reach the goal line is the winner. Chose a new leader and play again!

Variations: (1) Continue until everyone has crossed the goal line. (2) Once an athlete crosses the goal line, he/she runs back and starts the course over. Change the jumping pattern through a number of combinations: (3) right foot only, (4) left foot only, (5) both feet together, (6) bounding.

Equipment: Cones to mark the starting line

Lame Chicken

Objectives: To develop power and rhythm in jumping

Description: Place 10 Popsicle sticks on the floor, spaced about one yard apart, in an even row. The first athlete must triple jump over the sticks by hopping over the first stick, stepping over the second and jumping over the third. Once the first athlete has completed the jump, the he/she will begin again with the hop. After triple jumping over the 10 sticks, the athlete picks up the 10th stick and triple jumps back to the start over the remaining nine. Once back to the start, the athlete begins jumping over nine sticks. This continues until all the sticks are picked up. If an athlete touches the other foot to the ground or touches any stick, he/she has to start over. The athletes will not be able to complete all three phases on some jumps, depending on the number of sticks remaining.

Variations: (1) Athletes can jump in pairs. (2) Athletes can jump for time. (3) Conduct as a relay. (4) After the first athlete jumps over 10 sticks, the next athlete will jump over nine, continuing until all the sticks have been picked up. If the athlete touches the other foot to the ground or touches a stick, the athlete replaces the sticks already picked up and runs to the back of the line.

Equipment: Popsicle sticks (enough for all individuals)

Triple Bola Jumping

Objectives: To develop power and rhythm in jumping

Description: Stuff a tennis ball into a long sock and tie a knot in the sock just above the ball. Tie a 10-foot rope to the sock to create a bola. One athlete will spin the bola in in a circle. The bola should be swung so that the rope is approximately six inches off the ground. The rest of the athletes will stand outside the circle and let the bola pass them one time before they begin jumping into the circle. The first time the bola comes around to jump, athletes will attempt to jump over it, taking off of one leg simulating the hop phase of their triple jump. The athletes will hold their landing position on one leg. The second time the bola comes around, the athletes will use the step phase and step to the opposite leg as the bola passes and hold their position on the step leg. The third time the bola comes around, the athletes will jump over the bola landing on both feet. If the bola touches an athlete, while attempting to clear it, that athlete is given a point. The goal is to have the lowest score. If the athlete misses, he/she will start over again with the hop phase. After a designated number of revolutions, switch spinners.

Variations: (1) Raise the height of the bola they must jump over. (2) Continue pass the three revolutions, with the athlete starting off one foot for the step phase.

Equipment: Tennis ball, long sock, rope

Triple Jump Tug-of-War

Objective: To develop jumping power

Description: Form two teams with equal numbers. A tape line or rope is placed down, called the center line and marks a starting point. The first athlete from team A starts at the center line and does a standing triple jump into the opponent's side. The result will be marked (with a jump rope) where the heel of the foot lands (or the jumper falls back to). The first athlete from team B will then triple jump back toward the Team A's side, starting with the toes on the mark made by the previous jumper of Team A. Athletes take turns by alternating team triple jumping towards their opponent's side. When everyone from both teams has completed a triple jump, the winning team is the team that is in their opponent's territory. If teams are of an uneven number, make sure each team has the opportunity to take the same number of triple jumps.

Variations: Try using the following variations of jumping: (1) multiple triple jumps by one person each time they jump, (2) right leg only, (3) left leg only, (4) bounding.

Equipment: Tape or rope for starting line, jump rope to use as a marker

Distance Skip

Objective: To develop power and rhythm in jumping

Description: Athletes will skip for distance. The athlete starts skipping for five skips and the distance is measured. Progress to skipping for 10 skips and measure the distance. Progress to skipping for 15 skips and measure the distance. Add up the total distance skipped.

Variations: (1) If possible, skip on a football field and use the yard lines to help determine distance or mark distance on the jumping field. (2) Instead of measuring, start the next skip set where the previous one ended.

Equipment: Tape measure

Speed Triple Jump Bounding

Objectives: To develop power and rhythm in jumping

Description: Use cones to mark a distance 10 meters apart. Time athletes as they triple jump over a 10-meter distance. As the athletes become more advanced, move the distance up to 20 meters apart and then 30 meters.

Variations: Use jumping activities as repetitive hops: (1) left, left, left, (2) right, right, right, (3) alternate legs, (4) double leg hops, (5) bounding.

Equipment: Cones, watch

Triple Jump Team Tag

Objectives: To develop the power and rhythm of jumping

Description: Designate a playing area with two boundary lines 40 meters apart. A designated athlete will be the tagger and stands in the middle of the playing area. Athletes start at the boundary starting line and must use the triple jump technique of hop, step, jump to get to the opposite boundary while the tagger tries to tag them using the same triple jump method before they reach the opposite boundary. Those tagged assist the taggers. Athletes continue to go back and forth from boundary to boundary.

Variations: Use other jumping activities such as: (1)

bounding, (2) right leg hop, (3) left leg hop, (4) skip, and (5) two-foot hop.

Equipment: Cones to mark boundaries 40 meters long

Triple-Run-Triple

Objective: To practice triple jump technique in a relay

Description: Form teams of equal size. Designate two end lines 30 meters apart from each other. Half of the team will line up in single file line on one end line and the other half will line up on the other end line to run a shuttle relay. Place three hula hoops end to end in line five meters from each end line. On command, the first athlete in line will run to the first set of hoops and hop, step, and jump, landing each phase in a hoop. After completing the first set of hoops the athlete sprints to the last set of three hoops on the far end line and repeats the hop-step-jump into each hoop, and finishes sprinting to the end line to tag a teammate who runs back performing the same sequence. Continue for a designated time period or number of repetitions.

Variations: (1) Increase the distance between hoops. (2) Use different sequences of hopping and stepping in the hoops.

Equipment: Hula hoops, cones

One Stride Hurdle Hops

Objective: To learn the explosion required on the final jump

Description: Line up six hurdles four feet apart. Keep the hurdles low to begin with. The jumper stands one stride away from the first hurdle and takes one stride forward, bringing both legs together and squats with the arms behind the back and the knees bent about 90 degrees. The athlete throws the arms forward and jumps off both feet over the hurdle. Upon landing the athlete takes one stride forward and completes the same thing going over all six hurdles. The athlete walks back and repeats for the desired number of repetitions. As the athlete becomes more comfortable hurdling, focus on the athletes exploding over the hurdle and taking one step to explode over the next hurdle.

Variations: (1) Start with mini-hurdles or collapsible, soft barriers lower than 30 inches. (2) Start with one to two hurdles then increase the number of hurdles. (3) Time how long it takes to complete the hurdle circuit.

Equipment: Hurdles

Chapter 5 - Pole Vault

Watching a pole-vaulter fly through the air with fluidity and grace is an incredible sight. Pole-vaulting was initially used as vaulting over a horizontal distance and was a practical means of passing over natural obstacles in marshy places. Eventually the pole vault became an event of clearing a vertical height.

The object of pole vaulting is to clear a bar or crossbar supported upon two uprights (standards) without knocking it down. Initially, vaulting poles were made from stiff materials such as bamboo or aluminum. The introduction of flexible vaulting poles made from fiberglass has allowed pole-vaulters to achieve greater heights.

Physical attributes such as speed, agility and strength are essential to pole vaulting effectively, but technical skills are equally important. The pole vaulting games presented in this chapter are designed to familiarize the pole-vaulter with running with the pole and to increase approach speed. Many of the games are designed to work on planting and taking off. Since technique is highly important in the pole vault, some games have been designated for coaches and athletes to evaluate technique.

Safety in the pole vault is a primary concern. The pit should meet national standards with the standards properly set up. The poles should always be checked for integrity and only used under the conditions the pole was manufactured for. Use caution in adverse weather conditions such as rain, sleet, snow and excessive wind, which can all make pole vaulting dangerous. Pole vault coaches should always consult their specific rule book and follow the important information regarding equipment specifications and safety.

Pole Run Agility Race

Objective: To carry the pole and practice speed and rhythm in the approach

Description: Athletes will carry their poles practicing speed and rhythm in their approach. Set up a mini-hurdle agility course of 10 mini-hurdles about three meters apart from each other over a 40 meter distance. Vaulters will start standing up (like one would in the pole vault), carry the pole, and race over the 10 mini-hurdles. When the vaulters become comfortable over the hurdles, they can increase the speed of the run. Eventually, the vaulters will sprint the course for time. This activity will increase the confidence of the vaulters to carry the pole.

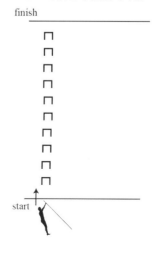

Variations: (1) Sprint a designated number of times trying to beat the previous best time. (2) Increase the number of mini hurdles with the hurdles closer together. (3) Increase the distance of the run. (4) Race three times against an opponent, add up each time and lowest time wins. (5) Sprint over the hurdles without carrying a pole. (6) Time the difference between running with a pole and without a pole.

43

Equipment: Poles, mini-hurdles, cones, stopwatch

Pole Vault Sprint

Objective: To carry the pole and practice speed in the approach

Description: Pole vaulters will race carrying s poles practicing speed in their approach. Athletes will race 30 meters holding their pole and using correct form. The time will start on the athlete's first move and will end when the athlete's body crosses the 30-meter finish line. Emphasize athletes running through the line. Take the best of three trials for a score.

Variations: (1) The vaulter will sprint the course a designated number of times, trying to beat their previous time. (2) Make the running distance shorter or longer (20 meters, 40 meters, 60 meters). (3) Time the difference between running with a pole and without a pole.

Equipment: Stopwatch, tape measure, cones, poles

Invert!

Objective: To practice getting upside down

Description: Each athlete will have a pole and will start with the tip of the pole against a wall. Athletes start standing up and slowly sit down with their drive knee bent, once athletes get to the position where they are laying on the floor with their drive knee bent they will start moving their hands and straightening their legs and turning over. This is all done on the floor. The athletes should finish with their right hand on the pole lying on their stomach, with their pole still pushing against the wall.

Variations: (1) Time each athlete and see how fast they can perform the drill, still having an emphasis on technique. (2) Add each athlete's time together and see how fast a time a team can post, trying to improve the time on subsequent trials. (3) Instead of using a wall have a partner hold the other end of the pole while putting pressure on the pole.

Equipment: Poles, wall, stopwatch, recording sheet

Plant Scoring

Objectives: To develop consistency in the pole vault approach

Description: Jumpers will take full approaches focusing on proper acceleration. The pole vaulters foot placement mark for the take-off is indicated on the runway with a mark. This mark should be the front foot when the vaulter takes off. This will be called the zero line. The pole vaulter will take a full approach run through. The emphasis is on running through the plant maintaining speed. Record to the closest inch or centimeter how far a jumper's toe is off from the take-off mark (zero line). A jumper can be short of the take-off mark or over the take-off mark. For example, if the vaulter is three inches short of the take-off mark with their toe, he/she will receive a three. If the vaulter is four inches over the take-off mark, he/she will receive a score of four. Take a number of approaches and add up the scores. Low score wins.

Variations: (1) Perform the game off of the runway. (2) Create a zone six inches either way from the zero line. If an athlete is within the zone, score is a point and out of the zone, he/she does not score.

Equipment: Pole vault runway, tape, tape measure, recording sheet

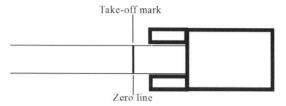

Take-off mark

Zero line

Horizontal Vaulting

 **Objectives:** To work on the planting phase

Description: Use a short pole (two meters in length) and a short approach run of no longer than 10 meters on a grass field. Place a hula hoop flat on the grass at the end of the run to serve as the location to plant the pole. Leave both ends of the pole open to allow the pole to grab into the grass surface. On top of the pole place five strips of colored tape at six-inch intervals starting six inches from the top to monitor height of the hand grip. Athletes should use the lowest grip possible. The athlete will take a short approach, plant and attempt to go as far as possible horizontally.

Variations: (1) When the athlete has completed three consecutive safe landings on two feet, the grip may be raised three inches. (2) Continue to raise the grip after three consecutive safe landings.

Equipment: Short poles, hula hoops, grass field, tape measure, recording sheet

plant

Pole Vault Long Jumping

Objective: To work on the plant and take-off while jumping for distance

Description: Using the long jump landing pit, place a hula hoop before the sand pit to serve as the plant area. After the hula hoop and before the sand pit place two pylons with a short cross bar over the pylons. Place hula hoops in the sand lined up end-to-end as targets. The first target (hula hoop) is placed one meter beyond the plant hoop.

45

The vaulter will use a pole two meters long or less and use a 10-meter run-up or less. The vaulter will take their approach and plant the pole downwards in the hoop near the takeoff line, forcing it into the ground and riding the pole over the crossbar. The athlete must land inside a target (hula hoops) placed in the sand. The athlete has to land with two feet in the sand. The pole must be grasped with both hands until the landing is complete. Changing the grip on the pole during the jump is not allowed. If target 1 is landed in, the athlete gets one point. If target 2 is landed in, then two points are given and so on. If touching the edge of a hoop upon landing, the jump is regarded as "successful." If, upon landing, both legs are inside the hoop, one additional point is awarded.

Variations: (1) Each athlete uses the best of three trials. (2) When both feet come down outside of a target, the athlete gets an extra trial to correct it. (3) Touching a target (side of the hoop) is penalized with one point.

Equipment: Pole 2 meters long, 5 hula hoops, two pylons, and small crossbar

Fly to the Moon

Objective: To practice planting the pole

Description: Athletes will use a full approach and plant the pole but will not swing up. The goal of the activity is to keep pressure on the top arm and to keep the bottom arm straight and pushing upwards. A partner or coach will keep track of how many times they keep pressure on their top arm and keep their bottom arm straight.

Variations: (1) Allow athletes to swing up on the plant. (2) Increase or decrease the length of the approach. (3) See how far athletes can push the pole by putting pressure on their top arm (measure where the athletes land in the pit).

Equipment: Pole vault set-up (pit, standards, bar), poles, bungee, tape measure

Rope Climb and Swing

Objective: To build upper body strength and simulate the body swing while vaulting

Description: Use a rope securely attached from the ceiling in a gymnasium. The jumpers reach above their heads while holding the rope and pull themselves up to the top of the rope. Once athletes can perform the rope climb, go to the next phase. The second phase of the rope climb helps simulate the body swing needed to lift the body over the bar. Include the landing pit at the end of the swing. Starting with the hands grasping the rope above the head, the jumper begins this drill about five strides away from the pit. On the approach, the jumpers swing their lower body forward and lifts the legs while arching the back. This will drop the head and the chest back. The jumpers continue to hold onto the rope. At the height of the jump while over the pit, the jumpers can snap their feet back towards the floor, or drop to the pit.

Variations: (1) Time the rope climb with each athlete trying to improve on the time over multiple attempts. (2) Perform the rope climb as a relay.

Equipment: Rope securely attached for climbing, mats below rope, landing pit

Technique Focus

Objective: To focus on one technique area

Description: Athletes will use a short approach (three, four or five steps) and attempt to clear a bungee cord or a cross bar. A three, four- or five-step approach may be harder than a full run for the athlete, because the vault will be slower, but it will help athletes use the correct form. Athletes will work with a partner. Partners will judge technique from 1-10, 10 being the best and 1 being the lowest. Athletes will be judged on the one technique item they pick they need to work on. Example: an athlete says he/she needs to work on rowing his/her top arm to his/her thigh. The partner will be only looking at and scoring that technique only.

Techniques to work on might include:
• Keep your eyes on your top hand
• Fast last three steps
• Drive your knee
• Keep your top arm straight
• Let your left arm bend after take off
• Keep your feet flexed

Variations: (1) The coach evaluates the technique. (2) The coach chooses what the athlete needs to focus on for each jump.

Equipment: Pole vault set-up (pit, standards, bar), poles, bungee

Jump On

Objective: To have fun and see who can clear the most bars with 10 attempts

Description: Every athlete receives 10 attempts at any height, with the objective to see who can clear the bar the most times. Athletes may choose what height they want to attempt. Athletes may stay at the same height the whole time or they can attempt different heights. Athletes may take as much rest in between as they need. As the athletes are attempting to clear bars, they will have a recording sheet to fill out, marking clearances and misses and one area of focus on for the next jump. Athletes are encouraged to challenge themselves and avoid continuing to jump at low heights.

Variations: (1) Use a bungee cord instead of a bar. (2) The coach designates the height instead of having the athlete choose. (3) Add up the heights of the jumps at the end.

Equipment: Pole vault set-up (pit, crossbar), bungee cord, tape measure, recording sheet

Name:	Height:				
X or O (miss or make)					
What I need to work on					

Name:	Height:				
X or O (miss or make)					
What I need to work on					

Go the Distance

 Objective: To enforce good pole vault technique

Description: The pole vaulters will perform a short step approach drill in grass to see how far they can go using correct pole-vaulting techniques. Athletes reach up as high as they can and that is where their bottom hand will hold, their top is then above that at the correct distance. Athletes will run and take four steps, lowering the pole at the correct time, planting it on the grass and moving their top arm straight down as fast as they can, landing in a lunge position with their drive knee forward. Athletes will measure from where they planted the pole to where they landed to see how far they can go.

Variations: (1) Land in sand. (2) Pole vaulters add their distances up over multiple trials.

Equipment: Sand pit, poles

A Perfect 10

Objective: To increase endurance and consistency jumping over bars

Description: Each pole vaulter selects one height he/she can consistently make. The vaulter will attempt to make that chosen height 10 times. Athletes will add their cleared heights together for a total score.

Variations: (1) Athletes can go from any number of steps they would like. (2) Use a bungee cord instead of a bar. (3) Keep track of misses and makes instead of heights. (4) If a bar is cleared three times in a row, award bonus points.

Equipment: Pole vault set-up (pit, standards, bar), poles, bungee, recording sheet

Pole Vault Gymnastics

Objective: To perform gymnastic drills related to pole vaulting

Description: Use a soft field or area with mats. Athletes will work with a partner. Athletes spread throughout the area and perform different gymnastic drills while the partner rates them in the movement. The scoring is similar to a gymnastics meet with 10 being the highest score one can get and 1 being the lowest. The partner rates and records scores. The scores of all the drills are added for a total point score. The activities to be performed are:
- Back extension rolls
- Somersault, tuck jump, straddle jump in that order
- Handstand push-ups

Variations: (1) The coach scores each athlete. (2) Each drill is scored individually. (3) The athlete performs each activity individually and attempts to improve his/her time. (4) Divide athletes into teams and each athlete picks which activities they want to do.

Equipment: Recording sheet, soft field or if inside, mats, recording sheets

Rings Make You Fly

Objective: To perform drills on the rings related to pole vaulting

Description: Athletes will take turns completing different drills on the rings. Athletes will need a mat underneath them to land on for safety. Athletes will perform different gymnastic drills while a partner rates them in the movement. The scoring is similar to a gymnastics meet with 10 being the highest score and 1 being the lowest. The partner rates and records the scores. The scores of all the drills are added for a total point score. The activities to be performed are:
- Pull-ups

• Pole vault swing ups

Variations: (1) The coach scores each athlete. (2) Score each drill individually. (3) See how many times an athlete can perform the activity. Example: How many pull-ups can they do at once?

Equipment: Rings, mat, chalk, recording sheet

Pole Vault Abs

Objective: To strengthen the core while practicing pole vault techniques

Description: Athletes perform various abdominal exercises specifically related to pole vaulting

Exercises:
  • The athlete lies on the ground with the drive knee bent and arms above the head. Using only the abdominal muscles and keeping the drive knee in front of the other leg, the athlete swings up to a vertical position with the legs straight above the body and feet flexed.
  • The athlete lies on a bench starting with the legs straight in the air. The athlete holds on to the bench above his/her head and slowly lowers the feet down to the bench.
  • The athlete lies on a bench starting with the feet down, only use the ab muscles to swing the legs up to vertical with the feet flexed. See how fast the athletes can get to vertical.

Variations: (1) Time each exercise and repeat to see if the athletes can improve their time. (2) Athletes may compete against each other to see who has the fastest time. (3) Make a circuit by completing each exercise as fast as possible

Equipment: Bench, stopwatch

Pole Vault Strength Circuit

Objective: To get stronger doing exercises that relate to the pole vault

Description: Athletes will hold their hands together with their arms straight out in front of their body. Athletes will step onto a box with their right foot, drive their right knee and jump up onto the box, then stepping back off with their right leg. Athletes then step on the box with their left leg, drive their left knee and jump onto the box, then step back off with the left leg. This is done with each leg five times. Athletes sit on the box and stand up on one foot driving the other knee and switch. Athletes do this on each leg five times. Athletes will place one foot on the box and step out with the other foot in front of them. Athletes will perform five split leg squats, jumping if they can. The lead knee simulates the drive knee while pole vaulting, and if the athlete chooses to do the arms over head, this simulates strong straight arms at the take-off.

50

Variations: (1) Perform the circuit with a weight. (2) Start with a light weight, then increase the weight. (3) Start with a low box and increase the height. (4) Do each exercise separately and time it. (5) Perform the circuit holding the weight above the head. (6) Emphasize proper technique.

Equipment: Various weights, boxes of different sizes, stopwatch

Chapter 6 - Jumps

All of the jumping events have commonalities that require the athlete to create a large force when leaving contact with the ground. All four of the jumps share the commonality of creating horizontal momentum on the runway or apron. Each jumping event requires the athlete to prepare the body for an advantageous take-off that will project the body into flight. During the flight, there are movements and counter movements that occur after take-off. Finally, the law of gravity says everyone returns to the ground for a landing!

In all four of the track and field jumping events: high jump, long jump, triple jump, and pole vault, the development of power, speed, strength, balance and dynamic coordination are vital to the success and enjoyment of the jumps. This chapter focuses on games that help develop the components that all successful jumpers in either the horizontal jumps or vertical jumps strive to develop. In training, athletes can practice these components to develop their jumping ability, and most of all, to have fun doing it.

Jump Tag

Objectives: To develop jumping power

Description: Designate the playing area to play a normal game of tag. Designate how many athletes you wish to be taggers. When athletes are tagged the first time, they must do three double leg hops before starting to play again. If tagged a second time, they must do three tuck jumps. If tagged a third time, they must do three bounds. Runners cannot be tagged while they are performing their jumps. Alternate taggers periodically.

Variations: (1) Use different exercises to get back in the tag game. (2) A tagger gets one point for everyone he/she tags. (3) Everyone has an opportunity to be a tagger for the same amount of time and compare the point totals of the taggers when the game is completed.

Equipment: None needed

Leg Match

Objectives: To develop power and rhythm in jumping

Description: Two athletes face each other and one is designated as #1 and the other is #2. Both athletes simultaneously jump up and down five times. On the sixth jump, they extend one of their legs. If both players extend the same leg, athlete #1 gets one point. If both players extend opposite legs, athlete #2 gets a point. The first player to reach 10 wins.

Variations: 1) Use both of the legs to take off. (2) Use the right leg only for take-off. (3) Use left leg only for take-off. (4) Emphasize jumping high.

Equipment: None needed

Kermit the Frog

Objectives: To develop power and rhythm in jumping

Description: One athlete is designated as Kermit the frog. The rest of the athletes are frogs and start jumping within a designated area using the designated jumping mode. Kermit jumps using the designated jumping mode and attempts to tag the jumping frogs. Once tagged, a frog become Kermit's helper and helps tag other frogs.

Variations: Use the following variations of jumping modes: (1) both legs, (2) right leg only, (3) left leg only, (4) bound from right to left, (5) double leg hop.

Equipment: Cones to mark the designated jumping area

Jumping Spiders and Flies

Objectives: To develop power and rhythm in jumping

Description: Designate the playing area boundaries. Two athletes are designated as spiders and stand on one boundary line and attempt to run from one boundary to another. The remaining athletes are flies. The spiders sit in middle of the playing area and the flies move around by hopping, bounding, or skipping. The spiders sit quietly and patiently until they are ready to leap up and chase the flies. The spiders are allowed to run. The flies caught become spiders in the next round. Once the flies are past the boundary they are safe and the next round begins. The game ends with the last fly being the winner.

Variations: Use the following variations of jumping: (1) two leg, (2) right leg, (3) left leg, (4) bound from right to left. (5) Start half of the athletes on one boundary and the other half on the other boundary.

Equipment: Cones to mark the playing area

Giants, Wizards, Elves Challenge

Objective: To develop power and rhythm in jumping

Description: There are three main species of characters, all vying for ultimate power in the forest. The giants stand tall and stretch their arms high over their heads and growl. The wizards have magical powers that come out of their pointing fingertips when they say "Abracadabra!" The elves have wriggling antennae-like ears (use your fingers wriggling above

54

the head) and are hypnotizing to any who sees them. Practice with each athlete imitating each character.

Each athlete will get a partner and face each other. Beginning at the same time, both partners will perform three vertical jumps. Immediately after landing on the third jump, the athletes imitate the character of their choice: Giants, Wizards, or Elves. The Giants beat Wizards (by stomping on them). Wizards beat Elves (by stunning them with their magic). Elves beat Giants (by hypnotizing them with their antennae). The winner of the challenge receives one point. In the case of a tie, each jumper receives one-half of a point. Jumpers are responsible for keeping track of their own points. Continue for a designated number of jumps or a designated time period.

Variations: Have partners sprint 20 meters toward each other. When they reach other, they high five and complete their jumps and the challenge.

Equipment: None needed

Banana Jumping Olympics

 Objectives: To develop power in jumping

Description: Designate two boundaries 30 meters apart. Divide into groups of eight to 10 athletes and give each group a banana. Each group will complete several series of different relays using its banana. Here are some ideas for those relays.

- The banana under the armpit and hopping on one leg down a field and back.
- Place the banana between the knees and hop down a field and back.
- Two teammates tossing the banana back and forth down the field as they hop down the field.
- Teammates line up in leapfrog formation and first player hops over the others while holding a banana and then tosses the banana to the next player in line to leapfrog.

Once a team has completed these relays, someone on the team is encouraged to eat the banana and the team that is done first is the winner. **Note:** Never require someone to eat the banana. It is often mushy by the time the activity is over. However, there is usually one brave soul who volunteers eat it!

Variations: (1) Run as shuttle relay. (2) Use your own ideas and add a few variations to the list.

Equipment: Bananas, cones to mark boundary

Jumping Bag of Balls

Objectives: To develop power and strength in the legs

Description: Designate a playing area. Empty or spread numerous balls around the area. These balls should be of different sizes and weights such as tennis balls, volleyballs, basketballs, footballs, and medicine balls. All athletes will start outside the playing boundary and run in to retrieve the balls. Each athlete picks up one ball and returns it to the bag using a jumping mode such as hop back, big steps back, or jump back. The athletes continue to retrieve balls until they are all deposited in the bag.

Variations: Use the following variations of jumping: (1) Two legs, (2) right leg only, (3) left leg only, (4) bound from right leg to left leg. (4) Start with all the balls in the bag and the first people to the bag get to empty it. (5) Assign points to different size balls.

Equipment: Bag of balls of different sizes and weights such as tennis balls, volleyballs, basketball, football, medicine balls, cones to mark playing area.

Rucks and Rovers

Objectives: To develop power and strength in the legs

Description: Designate a playing area with goal lines on both ends. Keep the goal lines within 30 meters of each other. Form two teams. The athletes for each team begin the game standing on their own end line. On command, players will move by running, hopping, jumping, or skipping trying to reach the opponents' goal line. The coach or leader calls out the mode of activity. Players will try to tag their opponent to prevent them from scoring. If tagged, players must run to their goal own line to start over. If a player scores, he/she receives a point and returns to his/her own goal line to start again and continue to attempt to score.

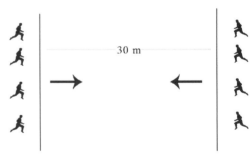

Variations: (1) Vary the taggers so everybody has an opportunity to be a tagger. (2) If tagged, a player joins the taggers.

Equipment: Cones to mark the goal lines

Indy 500

Objectives: To develop power in jumping

Description: Designate a loop course. Form groups of equal size. Each athlete in the group is given a car name—Porsche, Ferrari, etc. The coach or leader calls a car name. The athletes who match the car names, will run around the designated loop and try to be the first athlete back. The cars can have problems with a related jumping activity to perform. The coach can call out the problem, which initiates the start of the jumping activity.

1- Flat tire- hop on one foot
2- Run out of gas- skip
3- Steering wheel- run zigzag
4- Rusty transmission three steps forward- two back
5- Front end misalignment- double hops
6- Turbo boost- bounding
7- Yellow caution flag- tuck jumps vertically

Variations: (1) Play Indy 500 as a relay. (2) Each team is given a car name and the entire team goes around the loop together. The coach will stagger the starts or start the teams at different places on the course. (3) Place signs around the course to indicate the jumping activities to be performed.

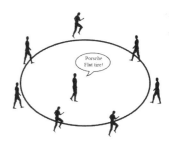

Equipment: Cones to mark the loop

Locomotion Tag

Objective: To develop power by jumping

Description: Define the playing area boundaries. Athletes will need a partner to play partner tag. Athletes will start the game by playing rock, paper, scissors with their partner. The winner will be the chaser first. The chaser designates the matter of locomotion and both partners must move in the designated locomotion. The chaser may change manner of locomotion at any time. Once tagged the partners change roles.

Variations: Different types of locomotion: (1) Hopping, (2) skipping, (3) crawling, (4) bounding, (5) running, (6) triple jumping, (7) add other creative activities.

Equipment: Cones to mark the playing area

As If

Objectives: To develop strength and power in the legs

Description: Athletes will take turns as one athlete at a time calls out "as if" activities and the remainder of the athletes will perform the activity. The activities should last 15-30 seconds with a brief (15-30 seconds) rest between the next activity.

Some sample activities for "As If":
Run as though you were going to run around the world.
Run as if Jason is chasing you with an axe.
Walk forward as if you're walking in yogurt.
Jump in place as if you are dunking a basketball.
Reach up as if you are painting a ceiling.
Step up as if you were climbing stadium steps to the top row of Yankee stadium.
Jump on one leg as if you were popping popcorn.
Bound as if you were a deer.
Hop as if you were a frog in a frog-jumping contest.
Shake your body as if you were a wet dog.

Variations: Numerous activities can be substituted.

Equipment: None needed

Rope Skipping

Objective: To develop power and rhythm in jumping

Description: Form teams of equal size. The athlete stands with the feet parallel in the starting position holding the skipping rope behind the body with both hands. On command, the rope is brought forward over the head and down in front of the body and the athlete hops over the rope. This cyclic process is repeated as many times as possible in 15 seconds. The athlete should hop on both feet. Every touch of the ground by the rope is counted. The best result of each team member is scored for the total of the team. Repeat for a designated number of rounds.

Variations: (1) Use the following modes of jumping: (1) Double leg hops, (2) right leg single, (3) left leg single, (4) hop-step-jump. (5) Score the rope skipping individually.

Equipment: Jump ropes for all athletes

Jump Scoring Tag

Objective: To jump across a field to a goal line and score without being tagged and repeating the procedure for a designated time period.

Description: Define the boundaries of the playing area with a starting line and a goal line 30 meters apart and at least five meters of running space outside each sideline. Form three to four groups with four to twelve athletes in each group. Designate one group to be the taggers first and they will stand at mid-field to start round one. All of the other athletes will start at the starting line. On command the athletes will perform a designated jumping activity and attempt to cross the goal line without being tagged. If tagged, the tagged athlete exits the left boundary sideline and jogs back to the starting line (staying outside the boundary) and immediately starts over and tries to score again. If athletes are not tagged before they cross the goal line they score one point and exit the right boundary. They jog back to the starting line down the right boundary sideline and attempt to score again. Each individual keeps track of the points that they score. At the end of the designated time for each round, the athletes of each group gather and total their scores. In round two, another group becomes the taggers. Continue the game until each team has had an opportunity to be taggers. Add up the team points from each round to determine which team scored the most points.

Variation: (1) Perform different jumping activities. (2) Add exercises to do outside the boundary once an athlete is tagged. After athletes complete the course, they will jog back to the starting line and go again. (3) After an exercise is completed, athletes do not have to go back to the start, they may enter wherever they exited the playing field.

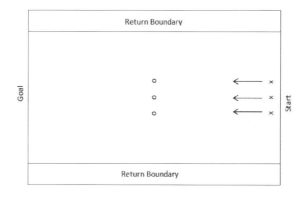

Equipment: Cones to mark the boundaries

Note: I often use four groups consisting of freshmen, sophomores, juniors, and seniors and adjust the groups according to size and ability.

Luck of the Draw Jumps

Objective: To perform jumps based upon cards drawn

Description: Form groups with four to six jumpers in a group. Give one deck of cards to each group. Each group member will take a card without looking and then turn the card over. The individual is responsible for remembering the card. Everyone returns his or her cards to the bottom of the pile. All members of the group will perform the tasks designated on each individual card for their group, including the activity and the recovery. When finished with the tasks as a group, everyone in the group draws a new card.

Luck of the Draw Jumps Activity	
Ace	Bound 30 meters
King	Jump on right leg for 20 meters
Queen	Jump on left leg for 20 meters
Jack	Jump off both feet for 20 meters
Joker	Triple Jump (hop, step, jump) for 20 meters
Odd number	Bound first 30 meters and jog 30 meters
Even number	Jog first 30 meters and bound last 30 meters

Luck of the Draw Jumping Recovery	
Heart	Rest 1 minute, return to start doing the same activity
Spade	Immediately jog back
Diamond	Rest 30 seconds, return to start doing the same activity
Club	Walk back to the start

Variations: (1) Perform as an individual activity with the athletes performing the exercise on their card only. (2) Individual athletes may take multiple cards at once and complete the tasks that are assigned to them. (3) Individuals take one card for the activity and one card for the recovery.

Equipment: Deck of playing cards

Multiple Choice Jumping

Objective: To develop jumping ability while having fun answering questions

Description: The coach asks questions (trivia, motivational, rules, etc.) and athletes respond by jumping into the correct position. The athletes jump three times and on the fourth jump they land in the position that corresponds to the correct answer choice. If the answer is "A," athletes jump and land with their feet together. If the answer is "B," athletes should land with their feet apart in a side straddle position. If the answer is "C," athletes should land with one foot in front of the other.

Variations: Keep track of the number of correct answers for each individual

Equipment: None needed

A   B   C

Chapter 7 - Shot Put

The origin of the shot put came from throwing rocks in battle and later from soldiers who hurled cannonballs in competition. The shot put competition for men has been a part of the modern Olympics since 1896.

The shot put involves "putting" (throwing in a pushing motion) a heavy spherical object as far as possible. The shot put is pushed away from the shoulder. It is not thrown like a baseball. Athletes take their throws from inside a marked circle seven feet in diameter, with a stop board in front of the circle. The distance thrown is measured from the inside of the circumference of the circle to the nearest mark made in the ground by the falling shot. It is a foul when the thrower steps on or past the foul line (stop board) or the shot lands outside the boundaries of the throwing area.

Emphasizing proper shot put technique and safety is crucial to prevent injuries. For beginners, it is best to use implements such as bean bags, tennis balls, softballs or light shots that are light enough that technique can be focused on. The games in this chapter focus primarily on the athlete obtaining a proper power position that develops torque and allows the athlete to use the body to throw farther upon release. Some games focus on becoming comfortable with the proper technique for the grip and starting stance and other games focus on the movement across the ring culminating with a proper release.

It is absolutely critical that safety rules are followed when instructing the throws. All throwing implements were at one time weapons of war and are potentially very dangerous when rules are not followed. Stress safety first to greatly reduce the risk of injury. Rope off the shot landing areas. Throwers should automatically check the area before releasing an implement. Athletes should always be aware when near the throwing area and never turn their back on an athlete about to throw. The coaches should enforce rules on who can be in the throwing area and how to return the implements. Throw coaches should always consult their specific rule book and follow the important information regarding equipment specifications and safety.

Note: The chapter on Hammer Throw games has several pertinent games that can also be used or adapted for the shot put.

Shot Bowling Bash

 Objective: To work on the release out of the power position

Description: Form groups of two to four athletes. Make bowling pins by using two-liter plastic soda bottles filled with an inch of sand. Set up soda bottles in the throwing area in the formation of bowling pins approximately 40 feet away from the throws release area. The athlete will throw from the power position and putt the shot towards the pins.

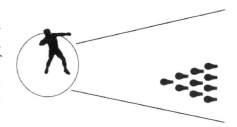

61

The other members of the group remove the knocked over pins from the area. The athlete then putts a second time. Score as a bowling game. After the first athlete has thrown, the next athlete will throw after the teammates have reset the 10 bowling pins.

Variations: (1) Remove the down pins and keep throwing until all the pins have been knocked down. Keep track of the number of throws. (2) Move the throwing line back. (3) Throw from the full position.

Equipment: Bowling pins, shot put, ring and throwing sector

Sponge Shot Put

Objectives: To work on throwing out of the power position

Description: Use a small dry sponge for a shot. Divide into equal size groups. The first person of each group will line up on the throwing line and put the sponge. Wherever the sponge lands is where the second member of the team will putt from. Everyone on the team will putt once. The team that has the longest cumulative distance is the winner.

Variations: (1) Throw for a designated number of times. (2) Out of the discus power position, throw the sponge. (3) Out of the javelin power position, throw the sponge. (4) For fun on a warm day, throw a wet sponge.

Equipment: Small dry sponges, bucket of water

Move It Back

Objective: To develop experience in moving backwards

Description: Many novice shot putters have difficulty with the glide in staying balanced while moving backward due to a lack of leg strength to execute the glide correctly. To give throwers experience in moving backwards and to develop leg strength, try the following:

Backwards running (timed for 20 meters)
Backwards hopping on two feet (timed for 20 meters)
Backwards jumping off drive leg (timed for 20 meters)
Backwards lunges (timed for 20 meters)
Backwards glides (timed for 20 meters)

Variations: (1) Add the total times for each athlete, low score wins. (2) Form teams and add up the individual scores for the team, low score wins.

Description: Cones to mark the 20-meter course

On The Line

Objective: To develop experience and control in the glide movement

Description: Form groups of two partners. The first partner lines up on a track lane line or on a football field with marked lines. The thrower will begin from the shot put starting position, push off with the back leg and glide backwards with the goal of placing the heel of his/her back foot and the toe of the front foot on the line. The thrower receives one point for landing the front foot on the line and one additional point for landing the back foot touching the line. The partner will check to see that the foot is on the line. The thrower continues to go down the line for 20 meters, scoring points for every foot touching the line. After 20 meters, partners switch roles. Continue for a designated time period.

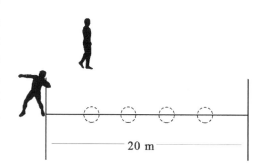

Variations: Time the 20 meters down the line

Equipment: Lines, cones

Towel Tally

Objective: To develop power gliding across the shot circle

Description: In the shot put glide technique, the initial momentum for the shot begins with a powerful backward thrust of the drive leg which projects the thrower across the shot circle. This initial push-off is important because it increases the horizontal momentum of the shot. The stronger the drive, the more potential to throw further. The "towel drill" will help throwers improve their initial push-off. The thrower begins in a starting position (facing the back of the circle). Place a towel 3 inches from the heel of the thrower's drive foot - the foot that's in contact with the ground and provides the force for the glide across the ring. As the athlete performs a backward glide across the circle, the athlete must push up and over the towel by driving the hips up and across the circle. The athlete scores three points for gliding over the towel and one point for stepping on it. **Note:** This does not have to be done in the shot put ring, as there is not throwing involved.

Variations: (1) Increase the distance of the towel from the drive foot. (2) For every inch the towel is from the drive foot, score one point for the thrower.

Equipment: Towel

Med Hoopla

Objectives: To develop power and rhythm throwing out of the power position

Description: Hang a hula hoop or tire on a goal post from a rope. The athlete starts one meter away from the hoop and throws a medicine ball out the shot put power position. The goal is to throw the ball through the hoop. Each athlete gets three throws from one meter away. Each medicine ball that goes through the hoop from one meter away is worth one point. The athlete moves back to two meters and take three throws. Each medicine ball that goes through the hoop from two meters away is worth two points. Move back three meters to take three attempts. Each medicine ball that goes through the hoop from three meters away is worth three points. The ball retriever will stand safely away from the throws and walk the med balls to the front of the line.

Variations: (1) Increase the weight of the medicine ball. (2) Form teams of three athletes with each one getting one throw at each distance. Add up the team points.

Equipment: Hula hoop, medicine balls, cones

Wall Ball

Objective: To develop power and rhythm by throwing the medicine ball against the wall

Description: The athlete assumes the power position in putting the shot while holding a medicine ball. The athlete positions himself one meter from a sturdy wall. On the start command, the athlete puts the medicine ball against the wall using a push action and catches the rebound. Emphasize using the legs, keeping the head up and extending the arms powerfully. Continue for a designated time or number of repetitions.

Variations: (1) See how many throws the athlete can complete in 30 seconds. (2) Throw in pairs, with one partner throwing and one partner catching. Once the partner catches the ball, the partner assumes the power position and putts the ball off the wall back to the first partner. Continue alternating putting and catching between partners. (3) Increase the weight of the medicine ball.

Equipment: Medicine balls and a sturdy wall that balls can be throw against

Knock It Off

Objective: To practice throwing out of the power position

Description: Form four groups. Each group will have a different set of six colored blocks or cups and several bean bags. Each team lines up on the throw line holding the blocks or cups. On command, everyone on the team runs up and places the cups or blocks in a pyramid formation five meters away from the throw line. The team runs back to the throwing line and each athlete picks up a bean bag. Bean bags are thrown one at a time using the shot put technique from the power position, in an attempt to knock down the blocks. When all the blocks are knocked down, the team sprints to collect the bean bags and blocks and then return back to the throw line. If all the blocks are not knocked down, and the team runs out of bean bags, they all sprint to retrieve the bean bags and return with them to the throw line to throw again.

Variations: (1) Move the block formation back to 10 meters and use the discus power position to initiate the throw. (2) Move the block formation back to 15 meters and use the javelin power position to throw.

Equipment: Blocks or cups to stack, bean bags, cones to mark the throw line

In The Hoop

Objective: To work on throwing out of the power position

Description: Design a throwing area with a throwing line and hula hoops. The hoops should be placed one, two, and three meters away from the throwing line. Place the circles far enough away from other groups to safely putt and retrieve the bean bags. Athletes will need a partner. Each group gets three bean bags. One at a time, the first thrower in the group throws from the throwers line using the power position of the shot put (see variations below for scoring options). After the first thrower has thrown, the group retrieves bean bags and the second thrower in the group throws.

Variations: (1) Score one point for the first hoop, two points for the second hoop, and three points for the third hoop. (2) Throw in sequence with the first throw landing in the first target, the second throw landing in the second target, and third throw landing in the third target. The thrower receives one point for landing the bean bag in the designated target. (3) Move the targets farther back. (4) Score points only if the athlete throws properly out of the power position.

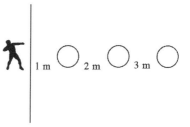

Equipment: Cones, bean bags, hula hoops

Team Shot Put

Objectives: To work on technique while throwing

Description: Form teams of three to four people. Each person on the team will receive three full throws. Add up all three of the individual distances on a team for a team total. The team with the greatest accumulated distance is the winner.

Variations: (1) Take only the best throw for each athlete. (2) Throw more than three throws.

Equipment: Shot put ring and sector, shot put, measuring tape, recording sheet

Shot Put Bingo

Objectives: To practice throwing while having fun playing BINGO

Description: Develop Bingo cards with numbers. Place cones with numbers to match the cards, out in the throwing area. Athletes take turns throwing and the cone closest to where the shot lands will be the number the athlete marks on their Bingo card.

Variations: (1) Use different variations of Bingo such as horizontal, vertical, or diagonal. (2) Play as a team completion.

Equipment: Shot put ring and sector, shot put, measuring tape, recording sheet**,** Bingo cards, cones marked with number to match Bingo cards

Better Marks

Objective: To work on consistently throwing farther every throw

Description: The goal of this game is to challenge athletes to be consistent with high-effort throws. Using markers to indicate the length of each throw can improve motivation and practice effort. Each thrower will receive six throws. After the first throw, place a marker to indicate where the throw landed. Individuals are assigned a number unique to them for their marker. The goal of the athlete's second throw is to throw past the first marker. A second marker is placed to indicate where the second throw landed. For every throw the athlete will have the goal of trying to throw past the previous markers.

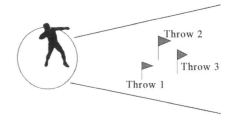

Variations: (1) For every throw that succeeds the previous throws, the athlete receives one point. (2) Measure the top throw after all six throws have been completed.

Equipment: Markers can be tennis balls cut in half, plant markers (available in all garden centers), plant stakes, etc.

Yarn Ball Toss

 Objective: To practice the discus throw release

Description: Provide athletes with a ball of yarn. Athletes stand on a throwing line. Each athlete must hold onto the end of the strand of yarn with their non-throwing arm and putt the yarn ball. How far does the yarn ball go? Measure the yarn from the athlete's hand to the spot where the yarn ball lands. The athlete should throw three times and to try to improve the distance each time.

Variations: (1) Throw from the power position. (2) Use a full throw. (3) If there are limited balls of yarn, take turns, measuring, and rewinding the yarn.

Equipment: Ball of yarn, measuring tape

Thrower's Golf

Objective: To throw the shot and attempt to reach a target in the least number of throws

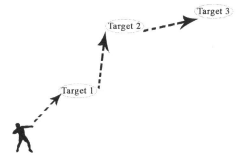

Description: Establish a course with cones as targets (holes) spread out throughout the course. Athletes will attempt to reach the target by shot putting bean bags. Athletes form groups of three to four. Each group will start at a different target. Athletes must throw using the shot put technique. The first throw occurs from a throw line next to a target (the tee) and the athlete throws to the next target (cone representing the next hole). The first athlete throws and will throw again from where the bean bag lands. Score the total number of throws to each target. The lower the score, the better.

Variations: (1) Vary the distance of the targets. (2) Increase or decrease the size of the targets. (3) Play as a team competition alternating throws. (4) Use tennis balls instead of bean bags.

Equipment: Objects to create targets (such as cones, towels, chairs), bean bags or tennis balls

Med Ball Frog Leap

Objective: To work on throwing power in a team environment

Description: Form groups of approximately four athletes. Each group should be spread out a sufficient distance to safely throw the medicine ball. The first thrower in line stands behind the throwing line and throws the med ball forward as far as possible with the designated method of throwing. One member of the group marks where the ball lands and another member retrieves the med ball. The landing point of the med ball becomes the throwing line for the second thrower of the group. The event is completed when the last member of the group has thrown and that landing point is marked. The team that throws the farthest is the winner.

Variations: (1) Throw for a designated time period and the group that throws the farthest is the winner. (2) Throw with a partner, alternating throws. (3) The entire procedure is repeated a second time (second trial). The team scoring is based on the best result of two trials. (4) Incorporate different type of throws: overhead, chest, side, etc.

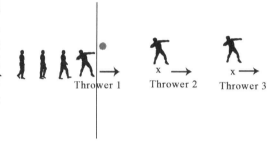

Equipment: Medicine balls

68

Chapter 8 - Discus

The discus was one of the events of the ancient Greek pentathlon, which can be dated at least to 708 BC. The discus thrower starts in a circle of 2.5 meters (8 feet 2 1⁄4 inches) diameter. The thrower takes an initial stance facing away from the direction of the throw and spins around one and a half times through the circle to build momentum, then releases the throw. The distance from the front edge of the circle to where the discus has landed is measured.

The weight of the discus generally ranges from 1kg to 2kg depending on the age and gender of the thrower. The discus is generally made of wood, with a metal rim and a metal core to attain the weight. For many of the games in *Track and Field Games*, a rubber discus is preferred.

For many games presented in this chapter, it is best to use implements such as bean bags, tennis balls, or Frisbees that are light enough that technique can be focused on. The majority of games in this chapter focus primarily on the athlete obtaining a proper power position that develops torque and allows the athlete to use the body to throw further upon release. Numerous games in this chapter will focus on the proper technique for the grip and release. Other games will focus on developing balance and becoming comfortable with the spin.

It is absolutely critical that safety rules are followed when instructing the throws. All throwing implements were at one time weapons of war and are potentially very dangerous when rules are not followed. Stress safety first and you will be greatly reducing the risk of injury. Rope or fence off the discus landing areas. Throwers should automatically check the area before releasing an implement. Athletes should always be aware when near the throwing area, and never turn their back on an athlete about to throw. Coaches should enforce rules on who can be in the throwing area and how to return the implements. Throw coaches should always consult their specific rule book and follow the important information regarding equipment specifications and safety.

Note: The chapter on Hammer Throw games has several pertinent games that can be used or adapted for the discus.

Discus Bowling

Objective: To master the grip and release of the discus

Description: A thrower must first master the grip and release of the discus. Discus bowling with a partner is a good drill to practice the grip and release. Each thrower needs a partner. Partners should face each other, standing 15 feet apart. The first partner holds the discus in the throwing hand, keeping the fingers spread apart. The first knuckles of the fingers should be over the bottom edge of the discus. The thrower bowls the discus along the ground to his partner, focusing on a smooth release that rolls off the finger. The athlete squeezes the discus out of his/her hand. It should come off of the index or middle finger, and spin in a clockwise direction for a right-handed thrower and in a counter-clockwise motion for a left-handed thrower. The athlete should try to roll the discus on a line, making sure to flip the discus as it is released. Focus on a fluid, rhythmical arm motion with a smooth follow-through.

Variations: (1) Move further apart as the athletes become more skilled. (2) Create a throw zone one foot wide and see how far the throwers can roll the discus before it goes out of the zone. (3) Score a point for every successful throw.

Equipment: Discus

Discus Bowling Bash

Objective: To release the discus while trying to knock down pins

Description: Form groups of two to four athletes. Make bowling pins by using two-liter plastic soda bottles filled with an inch of sand. Set up soda bottles in the throwing area in the formation of bowling pins. The first athlete stands 10 feet away from the pins and rolls the discus towards the pins. The other members of the group remove the knocked over pins from the area. The athlete then rolls a second time. Score as a bowling game. After the first athlete has completed his/her turn, the next athlete in the group will roll after the teammates have reset the 10 bowling pins.

Variations: (1) Remove the pins. Keep throwing until all the pins have been knocked down. (2) Move the rolling line back

Equipment: Pins, rubber discus

Discus Croquet

Objectives: To work on the release of the discus.

Description: Form groups of two to six athletes. In a field, set up a series of six croquet wickets by placing two stakes six inches apart from each other to make the wicket. Make sure the wickets are set at natural angles to make the course flow smoothly. You might use lime to mark the direction of the course. Provide each group with a discus. A rubber discus is recommended. The first athlete will roll the discus to attempt to get the discus through the croquet wickets. If an athlete misses a wicket, the team keeps going forward but receives a three shot penalty. To keep the game going smoothly, missed wickets are not replayed. The athletes in each group will alternate taking turns rolling. Add up the number of strokes it takes an athlete to make it through all the wickets.

70

Variations: (1) Play individually, if each athlete in the group has a discus. (2) If a group misses a wicket, the athletes are allowed to play back and go through the wicket.

Equipment: Stakes for wickets, rubber discus

Line Turn

Objective: To improve movement through the ring

Description: Athletes line up on the lane lines of the track. The athletes use correct discus technique and will turn on these lines slowly, maintaining good balance as they turn. Stress staying on the balls of the feet to allow the turns to be done rhythmically. Athletes can increase the speed on turns as they become more competent. Use a cone for the thrower to experience the pull of an object while they go through turns.

Variations: (1) Turn the line for 20 meters and score a point for each foot that touches the line. (2) Turn the line with a discus taped to the hand.

Equipment: Discus, lane lines on track

Slingers

Objective: To work on the release

Description: Each person will need a partner. Form two lines with partners facing each other five meters apart. Using a volleyball or tennis ball, the throwing athlete stands with his/her left shoulder (for a right-handed thrower) facing the throwing direction with his/her chest perpendicular to the landing area. The athlete flexes the right knee and lowers his/her hips and shoulders, bringing the ball back towards to ground. The athlete reaches out with the left foot in the direction he/she wishes to throw and unwind. Emphasize hips and shoulders rotating before the release of the ball. The partner catches the ball and then assumes the throwing position and returns the throw. Continue for a designated number of repetitions or time. This is a good way to introduce someone to the discus throw because it teaches the rotational movement without using a discus, which may be difficult for them to grasp with the hand.

Variations: (1) Move the throwing distance further apart. (2) Score one point for every successful throw and catch.

Equipment: Volleyballs or tennis balls

Hoop Frisbee Throw

Objective: To work on the release in the discus

Description: Spread on the ground, or hang from a goal post or tree a number of hula hoops. Each thrower will line up on the throwing line five meters away from the target and have five throws to throw a Frisbee, discus style into (or through) one of the hoops. Score one point for every Frisbee thrown into a hoop if the throw demonstrates proper discus throwing technique.

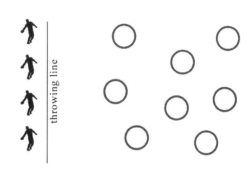

Variations: (1) Move the throwing line back a further distance. (2) Vary the game by assigning each hoop a different point value. (3) Throwers add up the points they earn for their five Frisbee tosses.

Equipment: Hula hoops, Frisbees

Rubber Chicken Throw

Objective: To work on the release

Description: How far can athletes throw a rubber chicken? Each athlete will use correct discus throwing form and throw a rubber chicken from the discus power position. Each athlete will throw from the throwing line and then all athletes will retrieve on command. Throw three times with the total of each throw measured and recorded. The rubber chicken will allow the athletes to feel the pull of the discus movement as they sling it.

Variations: (1) As an alternative, throw a rubber cone. (2) Form groups and total the scores of each individual member to have a team competition. (3) A partner catches the rubber chicken and uses the proper discus form to throw it back to their partner.

Equipment: Rubber chicken, tape measure

Range Throwing

Objective: To increasingly throw further at a certain percentage of an athletes' PR

Description: Set a PR cone at the athlete's personal best distance. Each athlete will have a different PR cone, identified by a unique color or number. Set a 90% cone 10 feet closer to the throwing ring. Set an 80% cone, 20 feet closer to the discus ring. Set a 70% cone, 30 feet closer to the discus ring.

Round 1: The athlete should be throwing at about 70%, which should be about 30 feet from the athlete's best. Throw three times with the goal to throw equal to the 70% cone.

Round 2: The athlete should be throwing at about 80%, which should be about 20 feet from the athlete's best. Throw three times with the goal to throw equal to the 80% cone.

Round 3: The athlete should be throwing at about 90%, which should be about 10 feet from the athlete's best. Throw three times with the goal to throw equal to the 90% cone.

Round 4: The athlete should be throwing at about 90-95%, which would be close to his/her PR cone. Throw three times.

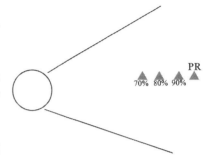

Variations: (1) Add a round five and go for distance. (2) Use a lighter weight in round five and challenge the athlete to throw past the PR cone.

Equipment: Regular shot, light weight shot, shot ring and sector, tape measure, cones

Flying Hoops

Objective: To work on the release in the discus

Description: Throwers will line up along a throwing line far enough apart from other throwers to safely throw a hula hoop. Set up cones spread throughout the landing sector. The throwers will use hula hoops and use a discus style throw and attempt to throw the hoops over the cones. On command, the throwers will all throw at one time and then retrieve the hula hoops all at once on command. Throwers score one point for every time they land a hoop over a cone.

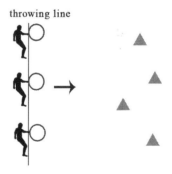

throwing line

Variations: (1) Start from a standing, power position throw. (2) Use a full throw. (3) Assign the cones a different point value.

Equipment: Cones, hula hoops

T-Ball Discus

Objective: To work on the discus release

Description: Form relay teams of four to eight athletes. Teams form single file lines facing the playing area. In the front of each line place a volleyball on a tall cone or a tee about waist height. On the start command, the first runner in line moves up to the side of the cone, brings the body back into a discus power position, and uses a discus arm movement to hit the volleyball off the

73

cone, simulating a discus release. Once the athlete hits the ball, the same athlete quickly retrieves the ball and sprints back to place it on the top of the tee and the next thrower in line steps up to hit.

Variations: (1) Develop a rotation from hitter to fielders. (2) Someone other than the hitter retrieves the ball.

Equipment: Cones, volleyball

Flinging Square Catch

Objective: To practice the power position of the discus

Description: Form groups of four with each group forming a square with an athlete at each corner. Each group gets one bean bag. The athlete with a bean bag assumes the power position in the discus and flings the beanbag to his/her teammate using the discus style throwing method. The throws should go in a counterclockwise direction. Continue for a designated period of time. If an athlete does not catch the bean bag, he/she should retrieve it and return to the corner of the square before throwing.

Variations: (1) Add another bean bag. Start the activity with a bean bag in opposite corners. (2) Add a third beanbag and start the flinging on command.

Equipment: Bean bags, cones to mark the four corners

Discus Freeze

Objective: To focus on throwing out of the power position

Description: Mark the playing area boundaries with cones. One athlete is the tagger and is called "Freeze." Freeze tries to tag as many of the athletes as possible. Once tagged, athletes must stop on the spot, start the discus throwing motion and freeze when they get to the power position. They hold this frozen power position until a second athlete designated as "Heat" melts the frozen athlete by tagging them. Once melted (tagged), the frozen athlete explodes out of the power position and simulates the discus release. That athlete is then free to rejoin the tag game.

Variations: (1) Encourage frozen players to call out for heat—"bring the heat!" (2) Change the size of the playing area.

Equipment: Cones to define playing area

74

Down the Center

Objective: Throwing the discus for accuracy

Description: Use cones to mark a center line in the middle of the throwing section. The thrower will be attempting to throw for distance and to have the discus land as close as possible to the center line mark. Measure the distance thrown in the normal manner and then subtract the distance the discus lands from the center line. For example, if the athlete throws 100 feet, but were 10 feet from the center line, the athlete will receive a score of 90. A foul will subtract 20 feet from the throw. Take three trials and take the best of the three. This is similar to the Punt, Pass, Kick contest football throw.

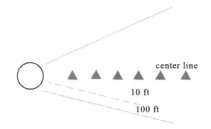

Variations: Measure and total all throws.

Equipment: Discus, measuring tape, marked center line

In The Zone

Objective: Throwing the discus for accuracy

Description: With cones designate a landing zone called the silver zone, five meters wide down and 25 meters long, in the front part of the throwing sector. Beyond 25 meters, create a gold zone 10 meters wide running down the middle of the throwing sector. If the throw lands in the silver section, a five-meter bonus is given. If the throw lands in the gold section, a 10-meter bonus is given. Each participant gets three trials, both being measured and recorded.

Note: As safety is critical in the discus throw, only designated people are allowed to be in the throwing (landing) area. The discus is only thrown when the "throw" command is given.

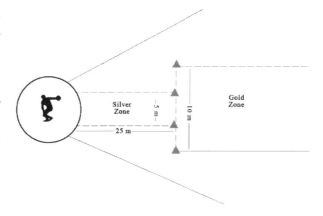

Variations: (1) Adjust the length of the silver and gold zones, depending on the ability level of the throwers. (2) Adjust the width of the silver and gold zones.

Equipment: Discus, cones, tape measure, recording sheet

75

Flinging Golf

Objective: To practice throwing from the power position

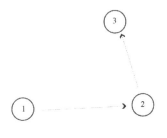

Description: Form playing groups of three to four athletes. Set up a course of nine cones similar to a golf course. Designate a starting point and call that the first tee. Athletes will attempt to fling a hula hoop from the tee over a cone in as few as tries as they can, out of the discus power position. Athletes will alternate turns within these groups and keep track of their own number of throws. Once successful, the athlete goes on to the next hole. Creative coaches can assess a "par" for each hole.

Variations: (1) Start groups of students at different holes to play a Texas scramble. (2) Determine par for each hole. (3) Lengthen the distance between holes. (4) Play as a team alternating throwing one hoop.

Equipment: Hula hoops, cones

Chapter 9 - Javelin

A javelin is a light metal spear designed to be thrown, historically as a weapon, but today predominantly for sport. The javelin length is between 2.2 and 2.7 meters (7 feet 3 inches to 8 feet 10 inches) and weight between 600 to 800 grams (21-28 ounces), depending on the age and gender of the thrower.

The javelin must be held at its grip and thrown overhand. The athlete is prohibited from turning completely around, preventing athletes from attempting to spin and hurl the javelin sidearm in the style of a discus throw. Javelin throwers have an approach runway that ends in a curved arc from which their throw will be measured.

For beginners and for many games, it is best to use implements such as bean bags, tennis balls, pool noodles, or Turbo Javelins that are light enough that technique can be focused on. The games in this chapter focus primarily on the athlete obtaining a proper power position that develops torque and allows the athlete to use the body to throw farther upon release. The proper javelin throwing technique is an overhead movement. Many games in this chapter will focus on the proper technique for the plant and release. Other games will focus on developing the balance and coordination that is involved in the approach.

It is absolutely critical that safety rules are followed when instructing the throws. All throwing implements were at one time weapons of war and are potentially very dangerous when rules are not followed. Stress safety first and you will be greatly reducing the risk of injury. Rope or fence off the javelin landing areas. Throwers should automatically check the area before releasing an implement. Athletes should always be aware when near the throwing area, and never turn their back on an athlete about to throw. The coaches should enforce rules on who can be in the throwing area and how to return the implements. Throw coaches should always consult their specific rule book and follow the important information regarding equipment specifications and safety.

Note: The chapter on Hammer Throw games has several pertinent games that can also be used or adapted for the shot put

Noodle Dodgeoodle

Objective: To focus on the javelin release

Description: Mark a playing area with cones. Form two teams. Designate a center line and two end lines. Each team gets half of the playing area designated as their side. At the end line for each side, set up cones three meters from the end line to form a jail. Each team gets three pool noodles to start the game and on command will start on their end line. Athletes must use an overhand javelin technique and throw the noodle to tag their

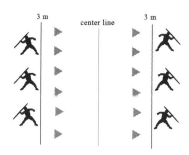

opponent out, hitting only below the waist. Once athletes are "tagged," they go to the other's team jail, where they can continue to throw at their opponents from the back of the playing area if a noodle comes their way. The goal for the game is to get all the players on the opposing team out. Focus on the noodle throw being overhead with good javelin throwing technique, not on how far athletes throw the noodle. Emphasize athletes to take a step forward when throwing. Athletes may not just touch their opponent with the noodle. It must be thrown. Either team may retrieve thrown noodles. Play until one team gets all the players tagged or until a designated time limit.

Variations: (1) Use more noodles for more activity. (2) Increase the size of the activity area for more running.

Equipment: Pool noodles, cones to mark the area

Stinging Hornet

Objective: To focus on the javelin release

Description: Designate the playing area boundaries. Four to six athletes will be designated as "hornets." Each hornet has a stinger (carries a pool noodle). The hornets will attempt to tag others by throwing the noodle at them using an overhand javelin throw to tag their opponent, hitting only below the waist. Once the "hornet" tags another person, the hornet loses the stinger (just like a real hornet). The person tagged now becomes a "hornet." If the stinger hits the ground without touching anyone, any player can pick it up and become the new "hornet".

Variations: A tagged athlete leaves the playing areas and performs a physical activity before returning to the game.

Equipment: Pool noodles, cones to mark the playing area

Noodle Target Throwing

Objective: To focus on the javelin release

Description: Use pool noodles or insulation for hot water pipes. These should be approximately one meter long. You may wish to cover the center 10 centimeters with duct tape to serve as a grip. Form groups of three to four athletes, lined up in single file line on the throwing line. Groups should be spread out about 15 meters apart. The front athlete in line will assume the power position in javelin throwing and throw the noodle (using proper javelin technique) at a cone placed five meters from the throw line. The thrower runs and retrieves his/her own throw and runs it back to the next person in line to throw. One point is scored for every time the team hits the target. Play for a pre-determined time limit with the team with the most points the winner.

Variations: (1) Adjust the target distance of the cone to suit the distance thrown by athletes. (2) When retrieving, the athlete who has just thrown throws the noodle back to the next person in line. (3) Throw and retrieve only on command.

Equipment: Pool noodles, tape, cones

Up the Rope

Objective: To practice the javelin release

Description: Attach one end of a rope (five to eight meters long) to a stationary object such as a wall, goal post, or pole. The rope should be approximately 1.5 meters high. Place a baton (or cardboard tube, or pvc pipe) on the rope so is slides along it. One athlete stands holding the other end of the rope at shoulder height, pulling to keep tension on the rope. The thrower assumes the power throwing position on his/her knees with the hand under the baton and throws the baton so that is slides the length of the rope. The goal is to see how far the baton can be thrown each time. Focus on improving the distance each time. The holder slides the baton back for the thrower to throw again. Throw for a determined amount of repetitions or time. On release, if the rope wobbles, the javelin was released too soon, or too late. No wobble on the rope indicates the javelin was released at just the right time.

Note: The goal is to simulate the optimal release angle of 30 to 35 degrees.

Variations: (1) When an athlete masters the shoulder height level, move the attached side up higher and the athlete throws standing up. (2) Take some throws with the non-dominant hand.

Equipment: Rope attached to stationary object, baton or cardboard tubes

Jamaica Javelin

Objectives: To work on throwing out of the javelin power position

Description: Designate a starting throwing line and a finishing throwing line 40 meters apart. Each athlete has a pool noodle and stands behind the throwing line. On the command to throw, the athlete will throw the noodle out of the power position and then sprint after it. Wherever it lands, the athlete picks it up and throws again out of the power position. Time how long it takes each athlete to get to the finish line.

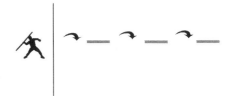

Variations: (1) Each athlete counts the number of throws it takes to reach the finish line. (2) Extend the distance between the starting line and the finish line. (3) Play for a designated time and see how far the athletes can go.

Equipment: Pool noodle, stopwatch

Javelin Pentathlon

Objective: To improve throwing power in multiple activities

Description: Each athlete will perform the following throws with the performances measured and recorded. Add up the five throws to get the total score. High score wins.

Overhead basketball throw
Standing overhead throw 1kg med ball
One handed – 1 kg med ball
Overhead shot put
Standing throw Turbo Javelins

Variations: (1) Conduct each event as an individual competition. (2) Form teams and add up the individual scores for the team. (3) Each athlete takes three trials of each throw and the best trial is used.

Equipment: Basketball, 1kg med ball, shot puts, Turbo Javelins

Cross Over

Objective: To develop the run-up with crossover strides

Description: The athlete will carry out several cross over steps in a side position, holding a Turbo Javelin or similar practice javelin. The athlete should hold the javelin steady in the direction of the throw. The focus should be on developing a smooth rhythm. Once the thrower becomes more comfortable with the cross over, time how long it takes for the athlete to complete the cross over run at varying distances.

Variations: Vary the distances used in the cross over run-up.

Equipment: Javelin, cones, stopwatch

How Close Can You Get?

Objective: To work on maximizing the full approach

Description: The goal is to get as close to the foul line as possible without going over. The javelin thrower takes a full approach run, including the cross over steps and focuses on proper technique. The thrower does not release the javelin. The distance from the foul line is measured in inches or centimeters. If proper technique is not used, the coach can call the attempt a foul and the athlete will get zero points. The winner is the one who comes closes to the foul line without going over.

Variations: (1) Throw the javelin and subtract the distance from the foul line from the distance of the throw. (2) Repeat for multiple attempts.

Equipment: Javelin, foul line, recording sheet

1 Step, 2 Step, 5

Objective: To practice throws from short approaches

Description: The javelin thrower will take a one-step approach and focus on throwing out of the power position with the proper release angle. The throw is measured and recorded. Each thrower takes three throws with the one step approach. Once all throwers have had three throws with one step, they move to the two-step approach. The focus is on setting up in the power position. Each thrower takes three throws with the three-step approach with the distances recorded. Each thrower will then take three more throws at the five-step approach. The focus on the five-step approach is on drawback and the crossover. Add up the best throw at each step approach. The goal is to have a high total.

Variations: (1) Form teams and add the scores of each individual to obtain a team score. (2) Vary the length of the different step approaches. (3) Continue throwing from more than a five-step approach.

Equipment: Javelin approach area, javelin, foul line, recording sheet

Javelin Acceleration

Objective: To focus accelerating all the way through the javelin approach

Description: The throwers will start at their take-off marks and use their full approach. The goal is to continue to accelerate all the way to the throw. The coach times the throwers from their first movement on the start to the foot plant of the throwing leg. The goal is to improve upon the acceleration time.

Variations: (1) Determine the distance for each athlete's approach run and divide it by the time for the approach. This will determine the speed of each athlete. (2) Compare the run-up speeds of the athlete.

Equipment: Foul line, javelin, stopwatch, recording sheet, calculator

Javelin Down the Center

Objective: To throw the javelin for accuracy

Description: Use cones to mark a line in the middle of the throwing section. The thrower will be attempting to throw for distance and to have the javelin land as close as possible to the center line mark. Measure the distance thrown in the normal manner and then subtract the distance the javelin lands from the center line. For example, if the athlete throws 100 feet, but were 10 feet from the center line, the athlete will receive a score of 90. A foul will be measured but subtract 20 feet. Take three trials and take the best of the three. This is similar to the Punt Pass, Kick contest football throw.

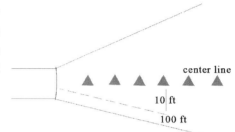

Variations: Measure and total all throws.

Equipment: Javelins

Javelin Snowball

Objective: A fun activity during snowy days that focuses on the power position

Description: Every year, the Norway National Snowball throwing champs are conducted with kids and adults throwing softball size snowballs over 80 meters. Have each thrower make his/her own snowballs ranging from baseball to softball size. All throwers will line up on the throwing line and throw at the same time for distance. Emphasis should be on the proper power position from a standing position.

Note: The athletes are not throwing at each other.

Variations: (1) Athletes take a full approach throw and throw from the throwing line. (2) Step off the distance and record in number of steps with the athletes trying to better their last throw.

Equipment: Snow

Beat the Hoop

Objective: To develop the javelin throwing motion

Description: Set up a field in the shape of a diamond with a home plate and three bases. Place a hula hoop in the middle of the diamond. Place three soccer balls by home plate. The first athlete holds the first ball overhead and walks three steps up to home plate and throws the ball in the field of play. The thrower focuses on keeping the ball high to simulate a javelin throw. The athlete should focus on continually moving forward (do not stop and throw), accelerating the throw by leaning back before the ball is released, and following through with a step or two. The athlete picks up one more ball and throws with the alternate foot forward (if thrown with the right foot forward earlier, throw with the left foot forward). The athlete throws the third ball in the same way. As soon as the third ball has been thrown, the athlete runs to first base and continues around till a fielder yells, "stop." Fielders cannot start gathering any balls until the third ball has been thrown. Fielders should stay aware of the other running fielders and balls. The fielders gather the balls and throw them to one of the fielders on the bases. Base fielders run the ball to the hoop in the center of the diamond. When all three balls have been returned to the hoop, a fielder calls "stop." The base runner will score one point for each base he/she passes before "stop" is called. Base runners keep track of their own score.

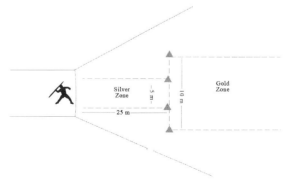

Variations: (1) Place targets in the field for bonus points if hit. (2) Increase or decrease the distance between bases depending on the ability level of the group.

Equipment: Three small to medium sized balls (such as soccer balls, cones, hoops)

In The Zone

Objective: Throwing the javelin for accuracy

Description: With cones designate a landing zone called the silver zone, five meters wide and 25 meters long, in the front part of the throwing sector. Beyond 25 meters, create a gold zone 10 meters wide running down the middle of the throwing sector. If the throw lands in the silver section, a five-meter bonus is given. If the throw lands in the gold section, a 10-meter bonus is given. Each participant gets three trials, both being measured and recorded.

Note: As safety is critical in the javelin throw, only designated people are allowed to be in the throwing (landing) area. The javelin is only thrown when the "throw" command is given.

83

Variations: (1) Adjust the length of the silver and gold zones, depending on the ability level of the throwers. (2) Adjust the width of the silver and gold zones.

Equipment: Discus, cones, tape measure, recording sheet

Medicine Ball Duathlon

Objective: To assess the development of throwing power

Description: Each athlete will compete in two throwing events. Points will be scored based upon the throwing performance. Record the points for each event and total the points at the conclusion. The goal is to score as many points as possible.

Standing Throw: The athlete faces forward with the medicine ball held overhead in two hands. Feet should be parallel and toeing the measuring line. Throw the ball for distance. A follow through step is allowed.

Three Step Throw: Start with both feet together in a stationary position. Take three steps forward with the medicine ball held overhead in two hands. Throw the ball for distance. A follow through step is allowed.

Light Medicine Ball:
The athlete performs a standing throw with a medicine ball (men 2 kg, women 1.5 kg). Mark the point where the medicine ball lands. Measure and record the distance from the front foot (on release) to where the ball lands.

Heavy Medicine Ball:
The athlete performs a standing throw with a medicine ball (men 3 kg, women 2 kg). Mark the point where the medicine ball lands. Measure and record the distance from the front foot (on release) to where the ball lands.

Variations: (1) Choose between either the light ball or heavy ball competition, depending upon the athlete level. (2) Perform both the light and heavy ball competition. (3) Compete in each event individually. (4) Score as a team competition.

Equipment: 1.5 kg, 2 kg, and 3 kg med balls, 30 meter tape measure

Light Med Ball

Points	Standing Throw Distance (meters)	3 Step Throw Distance (meters)
1	3.00	4.50
2	4.50	6.00
3	6.00	7.50
4	7.50	9.00
5	9.00	10.50
6	10.50	12.00
7	12.00	13.50
8	13.50	15.00
9	15.00	16.50
10	16.00	17.50
11	17.00	18.50
12	18.00	19.50
13	19.00	20.50
14	20.00	21.50
15	21.00	22.50
16	22.00	23.50
17	23.00	24.50
18	24.00	25.50
19	25.00	26.75
20	26.00	28.00
21	27.00	28.75
22	28.00	29.50
23	29.00	30.25
24	30.00	31.00
25	31.00	31.75

Heavy Med Ball

Points	Standing Throw Distance (meters)	3 Step Throw Distance (meters)
1	2.00	2.75
2	3.25	4.00
3	4.50	5.25
4	5.75	6.50
5	7.00	7.75
6	8.25	9.00
7	9.50	10.25
8	10.75	11.50
9	12.00	12.75
10	13.00	14.00
11	14.00	15.25
12	15.00	16.50
13	16.00	17.75
14	16.75	18.50
15	17.50	19.25
16	18.25	20.00
17	19.00	20.75
18	19.75	21.50
19	20.50	22.25
20	21.25	23.00
21	22.00	23.75
22	22.75	24.50
23	23.50	25.25
24	24.25	26.00
25	25.00	26.75

Chapter 10 - Hammer Throw

The hammer is a track and field event where athletes hurl a steel ball attached to a wire. Athletes throw a metal ball (16lb/7.26kg for men, 4kg for women) for distance that's attached to a grip by a steel wire no longer than 1.22 meters while remaining inside a 7-foot (2.135m) diameter circle. The hammer throw is an event at the collegiate and international levels and is offered on a limited basis with increasing interest at the high school level.

The hammer thrower usually makes three or four spins before releasing the ball. In order for the throw to be measured the ball must land inside a marked 35-degree sector and the athlete must not leave the circle before it has landed and then only from the rear half of the circle.

For beginners and for many learning games, it is best to use implements such as bean bags, or bolas (tennis ball tied in a long sock, with rope) that are light enough so that technique can be focused on. The hammer throw games in this chapter focus primarily on the athlete obtaining a proper power position that develops torque and allows the athlete to use the body to throw further upon release. The hammer throw technique requires a high degree of rhythm and coordination. The suggested games focus on developing the rhythm of the spins and achieving a proper power position to most effectively use the body in the slinging movement of throwing the hammer.

It is absolutely critical that safety rules are followed when instructing the throws. All throwing implements were at one time weapons of war and are potentially very dangerous when rules are not followed. Stress safety first and you will be greatly reducing the risk of injury. The hammer throw cage should meet the rules standards. Rope or fence off the hammer throw landing areas. Throwers should automatically check the area before releasing an implement. Athletes should always be aware when near the throwing area, and never turn their back on an athlete about to throw. The coaches should enforce rules on who can be in the throwing area and how to return the implements. Throw coaches should always consult their specific rulebook and follow the important information regarding equipment specifications and safety.

Serving Hammers

Objective: To practice the hammer throw by focusing on hip rotation

Description: Form two teams on each side of a volleyball net using the dimensions of a volleyball court. Each team is given two volleyballs. The goal is to serve the volleyball hammer style by tossing the volleyball with a two hand tossed released from beside the body (simulating a hammer throw) to the other the other side of the net. The receiving team tries to catch the ball before it hits the ground. Each time the ball hits the ground inside the playing area, the

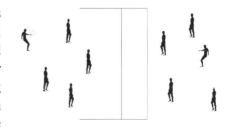

throwing team receives a point. As soon as a volleyball is retrieved, it can be immediately served hammer style back to the other team. If the ball is still in the playing court, it is served from the spot it is retrieved. If the ball is out of the playing court, it must be brought to the end line to be served. Play for a determined amount of time.

Variations: (1) Play two balls at once. (2) Play three balls at once.

Equipment: Volleyballs, marked volleyball court, volleyball net

Hot Potato Hammer

Objective: To focus on the hip action used in the hammer throw

Description: Athletes form a primary circle with their backs toward the inside of the circle. A medicine ball will be the hot potato. The potato is passed from one athlete to another around the primary circle. Focus on the athlete receiving the med ball in a power position with the upper body torqued and using the hips to deliver the medicine ball to the next athlete. When the leader yells "hot potato," the person left holding the ball is eliminated from the circle. After the second person is eliminated, the eliminated athletes will move to the secondary circle. There will be two athletes playing in the secondary circle passing the ball back to back. Emphasize full extension as they reach back to receive the ball and as they swing the ball in front of the body to hand off. Eliminated athletes in the secondary circle will re-join the primary circle on the next round. There will always be two athletes passing the med ball in the secondary circle.

Variations: (1) Instead of the player holding the hot potato being eliminated, change the rules every time as to who will be the hot potato. Examples: two people to the right, one person to the left, etc. (2) Athletes in the secondary circle are not eliminated and eventually there will only be one athlete left in the primary circle with the remainder in the secondary circle.

Equipment: Two medicine balls

Flip (Throw) Me The Bird

Objective: To play tag and practice throwing

Description: Designate a playing area. Designate two to six runners as taggers. The taggers may carry a ball to identify themselves. Make a bola by placing a tennis ball in an old tube sock and tie the tube sock. This is the bird. If a runner has possession of the bird, that runner cannot be tagged. Two to six runners that are non-taggers should have a bird. A runner who is about to be tagged can be thrown the bird (flip me the bird) before being tagged. The bird must be thrown using the power position and throwing hammer style. Any runner can handle the bird except for the runners who are taggers. If the runner is tagged before receiving the bird, that runner becomes the new tagger. Athletes should pay particular attention to throwers flipping the bird within a confined area.

Variations: (1) Once tagged an athlete must remain stationary until someone flips them the bird. (2) Use balls instead of the bird and throw from the hip.

Equipment: Up to six birds (tennis balls in socks)

Bombs Away

Objective: To retrieve a thrown bola and organize a line around the fielding team.

Description: Form groups with four or five runners in each group. Two groups can compete against each other. One group has a bola (tennis ball in sock). The first person in line tosses the bola anywhere in the area. The other team will be the fielding team and chases the bola. When the fielding team retrieves the bola, they must get in a straight line behind the person who retrieved it and pass the bola over everyone's head on the retrieving team. The thrower runs around the members of the fielding group, trying to get around as many times as possible. Every time the thrower goes around the group the throwing team gets a point. When the fielding team has finished passing overhead to the last person, they yell stop. As soon as stop is said, the fielding team becomes the throwing team and should throw the bola as quickly as possible. The person with the bola throws it anywhere, and the process begins again. Play for a certain amount of time and keep a cumulative total for each team.

Variations: (1) The fielding team passes the bola between their legs. (2) The fielding team alternates passing the bola overhead and between legs. (3) A volleyball can be used with the ball thrown from the hip to simulate a hammer throw.

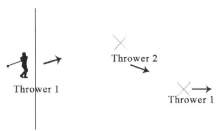

Equipment: Bola (tennis ball in sock)

Hammer Throw Leapfrog

Objective: To throw a bola down the field with a partner, alternating throwing and running past each other.

Description: Designate a starting line and a goal line. Two throwers form a group. Each group needs a bola. The two throwers will move the ball down the field by throwing it hammer style. From the starting line, Thrower 1 throws the bola. Thrower 2 (without the bola) sprints downfield and retrieves the bola. Throwers do not have to catch the bola but

Thrower 2

Thrower 1

Thrower 1

can pick it up off the roll. As soon as Thrower 1 throws the bola, he/she sprints ahead of Thrower 2. Thrower 2 will throw the bola as the two throwers continue sprinting and passing, leapfrogging each other down the field to the goal line.

Variations: (1) A volleyball or similar ball can be used with the ball thrown from the hip to simulate a hammer throw. (2) Continue back to the starting line and keep repeating down and back for a designated time period.

Equipment: One bola per two throwers

Hammer Circle

Objective: To practice spinning

Description: Form groups of four to eight athletes within a group. Athletes form a circle with a 16-foot diameter. One athlete (the spinner) stands in the middle of the circle with a modified hammer called the bola (tennis ball in a tube sock, tied to a 10-foot rope) extended towards the perimeter. The spinner begins to use a hammer throwing technique and winds with the hammer on the ground. Once the spinner has made one complete revolution with the bola, the athletes on the circle perimeter jump to avoid stopping the hammer. The spinner tries to make three complete rotations before being replaced by a new teammate. The spinner must keep the hammer within six inches off the ground. If the athlete is hit by the bola, that athlete receives a point. The goal is for a group to have the lowest score.

Variations: (1) Compete against other groups to see who has the lowest score. (2) If a group has a spinner complete three revolutions without being stopped, the group receives three bonus points. (3) A spinner receives one bonus point for every revolution.

Equipment: Create a modified hammer by making a bola. Place a tennis ball in a long sock and tie a knot in the sock. Tie a rope approximately 10 feet long onto the sock.

Target Hammer

Objective: To work on spins and release of the hammer

Description: Form small groups of approximately four per group. Spread hula hoops on the ground throughout the landing sector. Athletes will throw from the circle one at a time. If the hammer or bola hits in one of the hoops, the athlete will score a point. Repeat for a given number of throws.

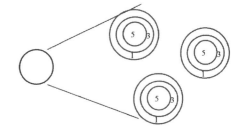

Variations: (1) It is recommended that a bola (tennis ball in a sock with rope tied to it be used. (2) Use a regulation hammer. (3) Use a concentric circle target, similar to an archery target and give different point values such as five for the center, three for the middle ring and one for the outer circle.

Equipment: Hammer ring, hammer, bola, targets

Hammer 500

Objective: To work on throwing out of the power position

Description: Create a bola. Place a tennis ball in a long sock and tie a knot in the sock. Tie a rope approximately three feet long onto the sock. Three athletes will be designated as the throwers and the remaining athletes will be out in the throwing sector to catch the thrown bola. The first thrower will yell out a point value ranging from 50-200 before throwing. As the athletes throw the bola, they will focus on proper technique on the hammer spin and release. The athletes in the field are spread out in the landing sector and will attempt to catch the bola. If the bola is caught on the fly, it is worth the point value that was designated before the throw. After the first three athletes get three throws apiece, rotate three new throwers in. Continue play until everyone has a chance to throw. Play until one athlete gets 500 points and then start the point tally over.

Variations: (1) Make the point value a consistent value of 100 points. The athlete with the most points wins. (2) The coach designates the point value before the throw. (3) Keep the group size small enough that everyone is active.

Equipment: Bola, throwing ring or line

Spins

Objective: To simulate maintaining control during the spinning action of the hammer throw

Description: Designate the playing area boundaries with two end lines. Form groups of four people. The groups will stand in single file line on each of the end lines facing each other. Place a bat (or similar object) in the center of the playing area. On command, the first athlete in line sprints to the middle of the area to the bat. The first person to the bat gets to go first and places his/her forehead on the bat and performs five spins (spinning the direction they would in the discus throw). After the first athlete spins, the athlete will run to the end of the line and tag the next athlete. Continue for a designated period of time or number of rounds.

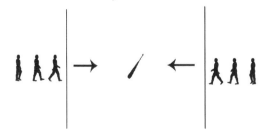

91

Variations: Every group has a bat to spin on. (2) Each runner performs a different type of spin: 5 spins on rear, 5 pirouette spins

Equipment: Cones to mark end lines, bats or pool noodles to spin with

Hammer Center

Objective: To throw the hammer for accuracy

Description: Use cones to mark a line in the middle of the throwing section. The thrower will be attempting to throw for distance and to have the hammer land as close as possible to the center line mark. Measure the distance thrown in the normal manner and then subtract the distance the hammer lands from the center line. For example, if the athlete throws 100 feet, but were 10 feet from the center line, the athlete will receive a score of 90. A foul will be measured but 30 feet will be subtracted. Take three trials and take the best of the three. This is similar to the Punt Pass, Kick contest football throw.

Variations: (1) Measure and total all throws. (2) Compete as a team competition.

Equipment: Hammer, tape measure, recording sheet

Chapter 11 - Throws

The throwing events share many commonalities in technique and training. In all four throws, achieving a proper power position and having separation of the hips and shoulders is extremely important for creating torque and maximizing throw distance. The hips initiate the delivery and are followed by the trunk. A nice high chest and forward position can be seen in all three events, as well as blocking the opposite side in order to transfer all of the energy through the body and into the implement. Another commonality important for every thrower is a high release point.

The shot put, discus, and hammer share a lot of similarities from the start. The tempo starts off slow and controlled and ends with an aggressive low to high finish. In the power position for the javelin, discus, and hammer it is important to maximize the length of the lever. The power position for the shot and discus is seen by having the shoulder facing the back of the circle while the hips are separated and more towards the front of the circle. The shoulders should be level for both events and the free arm (the one not holding the implement) should be long to create a stretch across the chest as the athlete moves into the release prior to blocking.

The games presented in this chapter can be used by all throwers to develop power, strength, and dynamic balance as well as have fun doing it!

Rolling Row

Objective: To practice throwing out of the power position

Description: Form two rows of athletes six meters apart with a one-meter space between athletes. The athletes will be holding one beanbag. One athlete or coach will roll a medicine ball between the rows. The first time athletes throw beanbags from the shoulder using the shot put technique to try and hit the medicine ball. The athlete receives one point for every hit. One athlete or coach on the other end stops the medicine ball and the athletes retrieve bean bags so that each one is holding a bean bag. Athletes retrieve bean bags when instructed. The coach or athlete rolls the ball back through the row of athletes in the opposite direction of the first throw. The process is repeated for round two except athletes will throw the bean bag from the hip as if throwing the discus. After the ball goes down and then back, round two is completed. For round three, the bean bag is thrown from above the head as if throwing the javelin. The emphasis is on the athlete getting in a proper power position to make the throw. Athletes should be advised to throw in front of the direction the medicine ball is traveling.

Variations: (1) Move the throwing line back. (2) Take multiple throws with one throwing mode (example: take five throws with the shot technique).

Equipment: Bean bags (one for everyone), medicine ball

Wall Target

Objective: To practice throwing from the power position

Description: Tape four hula hoops to the wall or hang from a goal post. The hoops should be three meters apart at about the same height as the heads of athletes. Form four groups behind a line three meters away from the hanging hoops. Each athlete should have a bean bag. Using the shot put style of throwing, the first athlete in line pushes the bean bag toward the hoop. Score one point for the bean bag hitting the target. Repeat with everyone in the group getting an opportunity to throw. Once everyone has thrown, the command is given to retrieve the bean bags. Move the groups eight meters away from the hanging targets. Start with the weight on the back foot and push the beanbag in a high arc, as far as possible. Continue the activity for the designated time.

Variations: (1) Use the discus technique of throwing the beanbag from the hip at the targets. (2) Use the javelin technique for releasing the beanbag overhead.

Equipment: Cones, hula hoops, bean bags, masking tape or duct tape. If you don't have beanbags, make your own by filling round balloons with dry rice or beans and then tying them closed. For alternative targets, tape two or three sheets of letter paper on a wall as targets. Draw circular targets on the paper for an added effect.

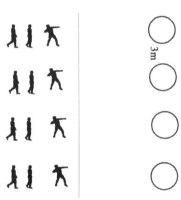

Water Balloon Toss

Objectives: To practice correct technique of the throws

Description: Form two lines facing each other so that everyone has a partner across from them three meters apart. Each pair will have a water balloon. Athletes on one side of the line will use correct shot put form from the power position to putt the water balloon to the athlete across from them, with that athlete catching the balloon. Every successful putt requires both athletes to take one step backward. For consistency, all pairs should toss and step back at the same time. Athletes continue throwing the water balloon back and forth. If the balloon breaks, then the pair is out of the competition and must do 20 shadow throws without the shot put. The last pair with an intact water balloon wins. If you run out of time and more than one team is still tossing, the team with the most intact balloons at the end wins.

Variations: (1) Use the discus throwing technique and throw the water balloons with two hands from the hip. (2) Use the javelin throwing technique and throw the balloons with two hands from high overhead.

94

Equipment: Water balloons

Floating Sticks and Stones

Objectives: To develop coordination of arms and legs working together

Description: Find an area that has a body of water such as a pond, lake or river. Have each athlete find one to two sticks. Form a throwing line and on command each athlete uses a javelin approach, emphasizing getting in the proper power position, and throws the stick in the water. Collect small stones for throwing in the water. Using the shot put power position, see how far the athletes can putt the stones. Using the discus power position, see how far the athletes can throw the stones. For safety reasons, emphasize all athletes will line up on the throwing line, at a safe distance apart from other throwers and will throw only when the throw command is given by the leader. The second part of the game is to use the shot put technique to try to hit the sticks with the stones. Athletes try to hit their stick but are allowed to hit other sticks. One point is scored for every time a stick is hit.

Variations: (1) All of the athletes attempt to throw at the same stick and see who can be the first to hit it. (2) See how many times athletes can skip the rock on the discus throw.

Equipment: A natural body of water such as a lake, river or large pond, small gravel size rocks, small sticks that float

Throwing Simon Says

Objectives: To practice throwing events

Description: The athletes stand on a line, standing five feet apart from one another without a throwing implement. The throwers will perform shadow movements. The leader (Simon) indicates a throwing activity by saying something like "Simon says do discus throws from the power position." After 15-30 seconds, the leader will change the activity by saying something similar to "Simon says glide across the ring as if putting the shot." However, if the leader does not say "Simon says" then athletes should continue the previous activity. Any athletes changing the activity when "Simon" did not say to, must jog around the group in a clockwise direction until "Simon says" to do another activity and then may re-enter the game.

Variations: Here are some recommended activities to do for the throwers. You can change or add your own. (1) Power position throws for shot, (2) Power position throws for discus, (3) Power position throws for javelin, (4) Power position throws for the hammer, (5) Shot put glides (6) Discus rotation through the circle, (7) Javelin cross overs, (8) Hammer spins.

Equipment: None needed

Hurry to the Hoop

Objectives: To develop power using medicine balls

Description: Form four teams. Form a playing area that is a square. Each one of the four teams takes a side of the square and spreads down the line. In the middle of each of the teams' line is a hula hoop to place retrieved balls in. If possible, each athlete should have a med ball, but it is not necessary for the game for everyone to have one. On command, all athletes throw the med balls at the same time into the playing area. The goal is for all the balls to be spread apart within the playing area. Players jog throughout the area but do not touch balls. On command, a team picks up a ball. The rest of the team will form a single file line and the med ball will be passed down the line, from the athlete's hip with full extension of the arms. After the last person in line passes, that person sprints to the front of the line to continue passing the ball down the line to place in their hoop. Athletes are not allowed to take steps with the ball. Teams can only pass one ball at a time. After placing one ball in the hoop, teams may retrieve another ball. The most number of balls in a team hoop wins.

Variations: (1) Heavier med balls get higher point values. (2) Pass the ball overhead. (3) Athletes run the ball back as individuals.

Equipment: Cones to mark boundary, med balls

Thrower's Baseball

Objective: To practice throwing out of the power position

Description: Athletes will play with a partner. Set up a target on the ground with four concentric circles. The inner ring circle, the bulls eye should be approximately one foot wide. A second ring inner circle is around the first concentric circle and is two feet wide. A third circle goes around the second and is three feet wide and a fourth circle is around the third and is four feet wide. Place the throwing line an appropriate distance from the target based on ability. This can be marked with ropes or other markers. Each partner will start in the power position and will "shoot" a medicine ball at the target using the shot put, discus, or javelin throwing techniques. Scoring is as follows: a miss (not hitting any circle) counts as an out, if the outer ring is hit, it is a single, if the second ring is hit it is a double, if the inner ring is hit it is a triple, and if the bulls eye is hit it is a home run. Athletes will play this game just like they would play a game of baseball, three outs then the next person will take their turn. While one athlete is throwing, the other will retrieve and keep score.

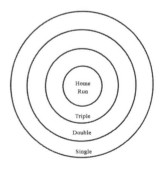

Variations: (1) Each athlete will have three attempts to hit the target and get around the "bases" as far as they can, and then his/her turn is over. When athletes have their next turn, if they left off

on "third," that is where they will continue trying to make it "home". (2) Make the target larger or move the athlete closer to the target to make it easier. Any adjustment made to targets must adhere to safety guidelines.

Equipment: Targets, cones, medicine balls, recording sheet

Knee Throw

Objective: To practice throwing using proper upper body position

Description: The athlete kneels on a mat, leans back (putting torque on the upper body) and heaves the medicine ball (1kg) using a two-handed overhead forward throw for maximum distance. After throwing the athlete should fall forward onto a mat with the follow through. The medicine ball should be retrieved by a partner and carried or rolled back to the throwing line for the next thrower. Record the best of three trials.

Variations: (1) Compete as a team competition, adding up the individual scores. (2) Add up all three throws for each athlete.

Equipment: Medicine ball, soft mats, tape measure, recording sheet

Overhead Backwards Throw

Objective: To use the legs in throwing backward for distance

Description: The athlete stands with legs parallel, heels on the throwing line and back to the direction of the throw. The medicine ball is held down at arms' length with both hands. The athlete squats down (placing a stretch on the thigh muscles) and quickly extends the legs, then the arms in order to heave the medicine ball backward over the head for maximum distance into the throwing area. After the throw, the athlete may step backwards over the foul line. The best measurement of the three trials is recorded.

Variations: (1) Compete as a team competition, adding up the individual scores. (2) Add up all three throws for each athlete.

Equipment: Medicine ball, tape measure, recording sheet

97

Over the Top

Objective: To work on the proper angle of trajectory

Description: Set up a high barrier such as high jump standards or pole vault standards with a cross bar. The designated object (shot, discus, and javelin) is thrown over the barrier. Four throwing lines need to be marked out: five meters, six meters, seven meters or eight meters away from the high barrier. Set the bar height at about 2.5 meters. The height of the barrier and selected distance from the barrier may need to be adjusted to achieve the proper angle release. The thrower starts throwing from the throwing line located five meters from the barrier. After the thrower is successful throwing three throws over the barrier from the five-meter line, throwers back up to the six-meter line. Continue to move to the further marks.

Note: Proper release angle for shot put = 40-45 degrees
Proper release angle for discus = 32-37 degrees
Proper release angle for javelin = 30-35 degrees

Variations: (1) Points are scored for each throw over the barrier (Throws from five meters = two points, six meters = three points, seven meters = four points, and eight meters = five points). (2) On each trial, a participant may choose to throw from any one of the four lines; potentially more points can be scored as distance from the barrier increases. (3) Score the throw as a team competition, adding up each individual athlete's points.

Equipment: Standards, cross bar, cones to mark throwing lines, throwing implements

Bean Bag Circles

Objective: To practice throwing out of the power position

Description: From four groups of athletes in single file, lined up on the throwing line. Targets are created two meters, three meters, four meters, and five meters away from the throwing lines by placing hula hoops end-to-end in line. Teams are awarded for throwing their bean bags into certain zones (i.e. two points for inside two meters, three points for inside three meters, etc.). Throw for a designated time or until a certain point value is obtained.

Variations: (1) Throw bean bags using shot put throwing technique out of the power position. (2) Throw bean bags using the discus throwing technique out of the power position. (3) The coach calls out the target hoop to throw to.

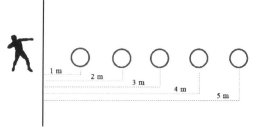

Equipment: Hula hoops, bean bags, cones

Hole in One

Objective: To practice throwing out of the power position

Description: Place a bean bag collecting bucket in the center of the playing area and have athletes form a circle around the bucket. Each athlete should be spaced around the circle three meters away from the bucket with a bean bag. One at a time, utilizing the shot put technique, athletes attempt to get a "hole in one" by throwing their bean bag in the bucket. Focus on each athlete throwing out of the power position and maintaining proper form. On command, athletes will retrieve the bean bags and repeat. Play for a designated time or until a certain point value is reached.

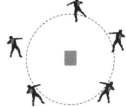

Variations: (1) The athletes all throw at one time on command. (2) Increase the diameter of the circle and use the discus technique when throwing.

Equipment: Bean bag, bucket for target

Throwers Trail

Objective: To perform different activities as throwers go back and forth in serpentine style on the throwers trail

Description: The coach will make three lines marked by cones and call them thrower trails. The trails will start at the starting line (trail head) and go to a cone that will be the turn-around point. Trail 1 begins at the far left corner of area. Throwers spread out with an equal number starting at each of the three trailheads. Throwers will perform activities down and back on the trail and then move to the next trail. After trail three, throwers go to trail one. This is a continuous activity. As soon as a thrower gets back to the trailhead, he/she moves to the next trail and keeps on going. On each trail there will be a specific activity. To help throwers remember what activity to do, post that activity on the cone at the beginning of each trail.

Trail 1: shot glide
Trail 2: discus spin
Trail 3: javelin cross-overs

Variations: (1) Vary the activities used on each trail. (2) Add an exercise zone at the end of each of the turnaround cones and perform a different exercise on each trail.

Equipment: Cones to mark the exercise stations

Run and Throw Biathlon

Objective: To simulate a biathlon competition of running and shooting (throwing)

Description: Form groups with two to four athletes in each group. Designate a loop course. At the ¼, ½, and ¾ points on the loop course, set up a biathlon shooting station. A shooting station consists of a line such as a jump rope laying on the ground (the firing line), two tennis balls and two empty jugs (a half-gallon or gallon milk jug works well). Set the jugs ten meters from the firing line and set two balls down on the firing line. Set up a penalty area from the starting line to a goal line (cone) 25 meters away and back. On command, the first athlete in each group runs to the first shooting station, picks up a ball, and using the shot put technique, attempts to knock down a jug by putting the ball at it. There are two balls and two attempts to hit the jug. For every miss, there is a 50-meter penalty run at the end. The thrower's teammates will be following the athlete and they will work together to reset the station by retrieving the balls and jugs. After the first station the athlete runs on to the second shooting station. At the second shooting station, the athlete stops at the firing line and throws two balls using the discus throwing technique from a standing position at the jugs. Again, the teammates help reset the station by replacing the balls and setting the jugs up. After the runners have been to the first two stations, they run to the third station and throw two balls at the target using the javelin throwing technique. Athletes then proceed to the finish line and run their penalty if needed. For every jug missed, they have a 50-meter run (down and around a 25 meter cone at the goal line). The next athlete in the relay group cannot begin until the penalty run has been completed. Repeat until all athletes have gone. First team to finish wins.

Variations: (1) All the team members go at one time and each athlete will have a ball to throw at every station. (2) Use one mode of throwing (i.e. shot) for the entire biathlon.

Equipment: Jump ropes, tennis balls, empty jugs, and cones

Note: The biathlon combines cross-country skiing with rifle marksmanship and is the most popular winter sport in Europe. Biathletes ski as fast as they can, then they must quickly calm down to hit a target the size of a half-dollar 50 meters away from a prone position and one the size of a coffee cup saucer from a standing position. For every missed target, biathletes must ski a 150-meter penalty loop, costing them valuable time.

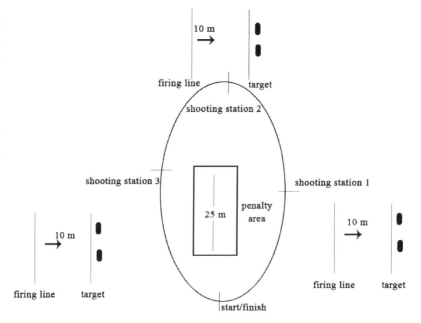

100

Frisbee Softball

Objective: To practice throwing the discus with a Frisbee

Description: Set up the playing area similar to a baseball field with four bases. Divide into two teams of equal numbers on each team. The objective is to score as many runs as possible in a set number of innings. One team will be up to bat first and the other will be in the outfield. **Note:** All throws by the offense and defense must be completed using proper discus technique. The batter up throws a Frisbee from home base to anywhere into fair territory and then runs the bases and tags the next team member, who runs the bases. The fielding team must retrieve the Frisbee and the Frisbee must be passed to everyone on the team. **Note:** The outfielders can't run towards the infield until after they have passed the Frisbee. The exception to this is that they may run if chasing a Frisbee thrown to them. Once the athlete on the fielding team has caught the Frisbee and thrown it to the next person, he/she runs to the pitching circle (marked by a hula hoop). Once the entire fielding team is in the pitching circle (hula hoop) the runners can no longer score. Count the number of runners that cross the plate as one run each. On a foul throw, the batter loses his/her turn, with the next person in line throwing. An inning consists of three throws per side and then teams exchange places.

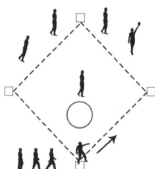

Variations: (1) Once the athlete who throws the Frisbee gets to first base, the next runner takes off. (2) Everyone on the team throws once before the inning is over. (3) Play with a soccer ball and all athletes use the shot put technique to throw. (4) Play with a soccer ball and throw overhead to simulate a javelin throw.

Equipment: One Frisbee, hula hoop for pitching circle, cones to mark bases

Luck of the Draw Throws

Objective: To perform throwing related activities based upon cards drawn

Description: Form groups with four to six throwers in a group. Give one deck of cards to each group. Each group member will take a card without looking and then turn the card over. Each group member is responsible for remembering their card. Everyone returns his or her cards to the bottom of the pile. All members of the group will perform the tasks designated on each individual card for their group. When finished with the tasks as a group, everyone in the group draws a new card.

Luck of the Draw Strides Activity	
Ace	10 med ball pounds into ground
King	10 shadow throws from shot power position
Queen	10 shadow throws from discus power position
Jack	10 shadow throws from javelin power position
Joker	10 shot glides
Odd number	10 discus spins
Even number	10 javelin cross overs

Luck of the Draw Strides Recovery	
Heart	Rest 1 minute
Spade	Jog 50 meters
Diamond	Rest 30 seconds
Club	Walk 50 meters and then jog back

Variations: (1) The individuals perform the exercise on their card only. (2) Individual throwers may take multiple cards at once and complete the tasks that are assigned to them. (3) Individuals take one card for the activity and one card for the recovery.

Equipment: Deck of playing cards

Throwing Boxball

Objective: To practice throwing technique

Description: Mark off an area of three boxes for every group of two athletes. The size of the boxes will depend upon the throwing ability of the athletes. One athlete will have an end box, the other athlete has the opposite end box, and the middle box is a strike zone. Both athletes stand outside their boxes and the first athlete comes to bat. The first athlete throws the ball (shot, discus, or javelin style) so the medicine ball bounces into his opponent's box. If it hits the strike zone or misses the box entirely, it is considered a strike. Three strikes equal one out. If the ball goes into the opponent's box, then the opponent must catch it on one bounce, but may not step inside the boxes. If the receiving player catches the ball after one bounce, it is considered an out for the throwing player. If the receiving player does not catch the ball after one bounce, then each additional bounce is considered a base for the throwing player. Two bounces is a single, three is a double, four is a triple and five is a home run. After three outs, it is the other player's turn to throw. The winner is the player with the most runs at the end of nine innings.

Variations: (1) Vary the size of the playing boxes. If athletes get good at throwing the ball, make the boxes smaller. (3) If athletes have difficulty scoring make the boxes bigger.

End Box   Strike Zone   End Box

Equipment: Medicine balls, boxes marked with chalk

102

Chapter 12 - Sprints

Sprinting is the act of running over a short distance at (or near) top speed. The first 13 Ancient Olympic Games featured only one event, the stadion race, which was a race from one end of the stadium to the other. Three sprinting events are currently held at the Summer Olympics: the 100 meters, 200 meters, and 400 meters. These events have their roots in races of imperial measurements, which were later altered to metric: the 100 meters evolved from the 100 yard dash, the 200 meter distances came from the furlong or 220 yards (or 1/8 of a mile), and the 400 meters was the successor to the 440-yard dash or quarter-mile race.

Sprinters begin the race by assuming a crouching position in the starting blocks before leaning forward and starting. They gradually move into an upright position as the race progresses and momentum is gained. Many of the games presented in this chapter help develop the use of an effective start. Sprint development in some of the games are largely focused upon acceleration to an athlete's maximum speed and other games emphasize the maintenance of maximum speed and obtaining speed endurance.

Safety in track and field is always a priority. Care should be taken that athletes are warmed up properly before engaging in high intensity running. Careful planning on defining boundaries for sprinting games are important and instruction on running in lanes is valuable on minimizing collision and injuries. Track and field coaches should always consult their specific rule book regarding proper facilities and equipment and follow the important information regarding equipment specifications and safety.

Sprint Warm-up

Objective: To warm-up

Description: Designate a playing area with boundaries. Athletes will play tag using multiple agilities. Two people will be taggers and they will call out when to switch agilities. Everyone will do the agility called out. After a designated period of time, switch taggers.

Agility Examples:

- Walking lunges
- Tin man
- Walking hamstring
- Knee hugs
- Side lunges
- Heel walk
- Toe walk
- Walking quad pulls
- High knees
- Butt kicks
- A skips
- B skips

Variations: (1) The activity may be completed using only one agility. (2) The activity may be played as a relay race instead of tag. (3) Adjust the number of taggers and vary the size of the playing field to make the activity appropriate to the athlete level.

Equipment: Cones to mark the playing area

Armless Challenge

Objectives: To focus attention on the use of the arms during running

Description: Identify a 60- to 100-meter uphill area to safely sprint up. The first sprint up the hill is performed with the athletes holding their arms behind their back and running full speed up the hill. The time for each athlete is recorded. The athlete is allowed a sufficient amount of time to go back down the hill and recover. The second sprint is ran with a normal sprinting action, focusing on good arm action. The time for the second sprint is recorded. The athlete compares the time between not using the arms and using the arms. Repeat the activity three to five times. The athletes should note the differences in comfort, power, and speed in armless running versus normal running.

Variations: (1) Athletes restrain the arm swing by carrying two small cups, each filled halfway with water. (2) Have the athletes try to balance tennis balls on big spoons in each hand as they sprint up the hill.

Equipment: Cones to mark the sprinting area, stopwatch, recording sheet

Calculating Stride Length

Objective: To examine the role of stride length in sprinting

Description:
Walking: The athlete walks a normal pace over 100 meters and counts the number of steps taken. To calculate stride length, divide 100 by the number of steps the athlete takes. For example, if the athlete takes 40 steps to cover the 100 meters, the stride length will be 100 meters divided by 80, which equals 1.25 meters per stride. Another way to measure stride length is to walk through a water puddle onto dry pavement and measure the heel-to-heel distance of the wet footprints.

Jogging: The athlete jogs over 100 meters and counts the number of steps taken. To calculate stride length, divide 100 by the number of steps taken. For example, if it takes 60 steps to cover the 100 meters, the stride length will be 100 meters divided by 60, which equals 1.66 meters per stride.

Sprinting: The athlete sprints over 100 meters and counts the number of steps taken. To calculate stride length, divide 100 by the number of steps taken. For example, if it takes 40 steps to cover the 100 meters, the stride length will be 100 meters divided by 40, which equals 2.25 meters per stride.

Have the athlete compare the stride length at different speeds. Stride length and stride frequency are the two major components of increasing speed and running faster. Increasing stride length is achieved by resistance training methods such as flexibility, plyometrics, weight training, running up-hill, and pulling weighted objects.

Variations: Convert steps to mileage. (1) Walk for a designated period of time and count the steps. Have the athletes multiply the number of steps by their stride length to determine how far they have walked. (2) Jog for a designated period of time and count the steps. Have the athletes multiply the number of steps by their stride length to determine how far they have jogged. (3) Sprint for a designated period of time and count the steps. Have the athletes multiply the number of steps by their stride length to determine how far they have sprinted.

Equipment: Tape measure, stopwatch

Check My Speed (with radar gun)

Objective: To determine how fast runners run by doing a speed check

Description: After a sufficient warm-up, each runner runs alone for 50 meters all out and a radar gun is used to measure top speed. Give each runner a recovery period (this can be done while waiting for others to go). Each runner runs four times and their top speed in miles per hour up is added up. If someone runs 16 mph, 15 mph, 14 mph, and 15 mph, that would total 60.

Variations: (1) Use a fly zone of 20 meters in an attempt to hit maximum speed.

Equipment: Radar gun (try borrowing from baseball or softball teams)

Note: While running down the road one morning, I noticed the police had set up a portable radar display that indicated how fast cars were traveling down the street. No cars were in sight and it read 12. I realized that was my speed! That day at practice, I took the team over to check our speed and they had a blast. They ran along the side of the road in the park to see what their maximum speed was. They wanted to go over and over again to get a faster and higher speed, and I enthusiastically encouraged them to do so. You can only hope the police department sets up a radar display in your neighborhood, or you can borrow a radar gun from the baseball or softball teams to use.

Starting Circle

Objective: To practice starts

Description: Two teams are placed in a large circle with at least a 30-meter diameter. Each team member has a number. Teams are arranged so that the same number on the opposite team will be facing each other. Each team has a team object specific to that team (such as tennis ball, rubber chicken, etc.) placed in the middle of the circle. The coach or leader will use the following format when calling off numbers. "Runners to your marks." At this command, all runners on the circle will take their marks from a sprinter starting position. No starting blocks will be used for this activity. When the coach or leader commands "set," all runners come up to a set position. The coach or leader will now call out a number which is the command for the two runners who have that number to start and sprint to the inside of the circle, grab their object, run back through their position they vacated, run the circle clockwise, return through their spot and place the object back in the center. Arrange to have students of equal ability paired against each other. Repeat until everyone has had a chance to start and run.

Variations: (1) Runners use a stand up start and commands are race starting commands. "Runners set" and all runners assume a stand up starting position. On the number command, the two runners whose numbers are called will sprint and perform the starting wheel activity. (2) Place only one object in the middle of the circle and when the command is given, the two starters race for the object. (3) Vary the length of the start by increasing the diameter of the circle.

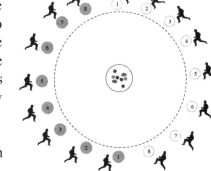

Equipment: Use different objects that are safe for teams to run with such as a tennis ball and rubber chicken.

Spin and Start

Objective: To practice coming out of the starting position

Description: Athletes jog slowly in a straight line and at the coach's whistle, the athlete jumps in the air and turns around 180 degrees and immediately falls into a starting "set" position. This starting position is only held for one second before the runner accelerates and sprints for 10 meters. After sprinting, the athletes begin jogging slowly again in a straight line. Coaches should give the athlete time to recover before repeating the spin and start. Continue for a designated number of times.

Variations: (1) Athletes assume the start "set" position for five seconds and then stand up and begin jogging (they do not sprint out). (2) Athletes go down into the "on your marks" position, hold it for three seconds, come into the "set" position, which they hold for one second and then accelerate out of that position. (3) Athletes come up to the set position and then start on the coach's command.

Equipment: Whistle

Starting Ladder

Objective: Working on the start and the first few steps out of the blocks

Description: The athlete will work on the start by coming out of the starting blocks on command and running five meters at full speed. Encourage the athlete to run hard past the five meter mark, as there is a tendency to slow down before the end. The coach or a partner times the athlete. The second time out of the blocks, the athlete is timed for the first 10 meters. Progress to 15, then 20, then 25 meters. Add up the times of all five starts and compare to other athletes.

Variations: (1) Run the starts again and try to beat your times. (2) Run as a team competition by adding up the individual times for a team score.

Equipment: Starting blocks, stopwatch, recording sheet

Bean Bag Start

Objective: To improve the arm action in the start out of the blocks

Description: The athlete assumes the starting position in the blocks. A partner will place one bean bag on top of the right hand and one bean bag on top of the left hand. When the gun fires or the command "go" is given, the athlete drives the arms hard coming out of the blocks. The arm opposite the front step will fly forward vigorously throwing the bean bag forward. The arm opposite the back foot forward will vigorously throw the bean bag backwards. The athlete takes a couple of steps out of the blocks, stops and returns to the blocks. Challenge athletes to see how far they can throw the beanbags.

Variations: (1) Measure how far athletes can throw the bean bags. (2) Increase the number of steps the athlete takes out of the blocks.

Equipment: Starting blocks, bean bags

Leaping Start

Objective: To improve the arm action in the start out of the blocks

Description: Place the starting blocks in front of the landing area (sand) at the long jump pit. When the commands are given the athlete takes their marks and then comes up to the set position. When the command "go" is given, or gun fired, the athletes drive the arms and legs hard and thrust themselves into the sand. The goal of the athletes is to see how far they can thrust

themselves into the sand. The athletes wipe the sand off themselves and re-positions in the starting blocks to go again. The goal is to keep going farther and farther in the sand.

Variations: (1) Measure how far the athlete can reach in the sand. Measure from where the back foot lands to the blocks. (2) Conduct a team competition with the team totals added up.

Equipment: Starting blocks, long jump pit, tape measure

King of the Mountain

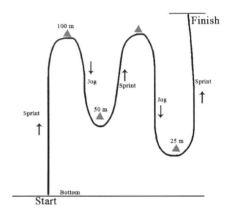

Objectives: To work on uphill running

Description: Select a hill that has a fairly good incline but not too long. Set up cones 100, 50 and 25 meters up from the bottom of the hill. The runners start at the cone at the bottom of the hill and sprint up to the 100-meter cone, turn around and jog back down to the 50-meter cone, turn around and sprint up the hill again to the 100-meter cone and jog back down to the 25-meter cone. One more time, they sprint to the top of the hill to finish the circuit.

Variations: (1) When a runner can complete the circuit without walking, he/she earns a point. Runners continue to get a point for every completion of the circuit. Four points earns the honorary title King on the Mountain. (2) Play for a designated time period. (3) Increase the difficulty by completing the circuit by running back to the starting line before one final time up the hill.

Equipment: Cones

Ah Race

Objective: To see how far athletes can sprint while holding their breath

Description: Mark a running area with a cone placed every 10 meters up to 100 meters or run on a football field. Each athlete begins running and can take only one breath. Each athlete will yell "Ahhhhhhhhhhh" when they start running and continue yelling until they have to take a breath. Once the athlete has to take a breath and quit yelling, that round is over for the athlete. If an athlete hits the 100-meter mark and is still "ahhhing," he/she turns around and continues back. One point is awarded for every 10 meters the athlete can run. Athletes perform another round and see if they can better their performance. Continue for a designated number of rounds to see how many points can be scored.

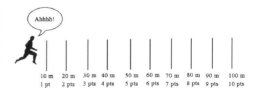

Variation: Perform a relay competition with the team in single file line jogging. The first runner starts screaming while running and when he/she can no longer scream, the second runner in line starts screaming with the first runner moving to the back of the single file jogging line.

Equipment: Cones to mark every 10 meters

Fly Zone Challenge

Objectives: To develop running at full speed

Description: Designate a starting line. Thirty meters down the track, set one cone and set another cone 30 meters down the track from the first cone. The 30 meters between the cones is referred to as the "fly zone." The athlete will start from the starting line and use a gradual acceleration phase to build up to the first cone. The athlete should be at high velocity by the time he/she enters the fly zone. The athlete is timed in the fly zone, beginning when he/she passes the first cone and ending on passing the second cone. Emphasize the athlete running past the second cone and out of the fly zone before deceleration. Allow for a full recovery and repeat a designated number of times. Challenge the athletes to run the times as consistent as possible.

Variations: (1) Score the fly zone challenge. The first timed fly zone time is set as the standard. Every succeeding fly zone time should match the first one. For every tenth of a second the time is faster, the sprinter receives a point. For every tenth of a second slower, one point is deducted. (2) If a sprinter runs a faster time than the established standard, then that time will become the established standard on the next fly zone run.

accelerate   30 m
Fly Zone   decelerate

Equipment: Cones, stopwatch, recording sheet

Photo Finish

Objective: To use a picture to determine which team can have the closest finish.

Photographer

Description: Divide into groups with approximately five runners in each group. Each group will need a digital camera. Designate one of the group members to be the photographer for the first round. The other four people in the group will run a designated distance (approximately 100 meters). The objective is to have all of the runners in the group abreast at the finish line, with the photographer taking a picture, a photo finish. After crossing the finish line, the runners jog back to the starting line. In the second round, rotate so another runner in the group is the photographer. Continuing rotating so each person in the group will have a chance to be the photographer. Within each group determine which running round had the

109

closest finish (everybody in the group together leaning across the line). Groups should compare their closest finish picture to the other groups to determine who had the "closest" overall photo finish.

Variations: (1) Runners perform the run all out. (2) The runners or coach can set a goal pace that everyone on the team is capable of running.

Equipment: Digital photo camera or cell phone camera for each team

Synchronized Sprinting

Objective: To have all runners synchronizing their arms and legs as they run

Description: Divide into groups of four to eight runners per group. The runners in each group line up side by side in a straight line and attempt to synchronize their arms and legs as they run. Start off running a straight line, such as a track straightaway. Runners should run at a slow speed the first few times to practice before they gradually pick up the pace. After a straight line run is mastered, the runners should attempt to run a curve. Place the faster runners on the outside, as they will be running further. It takes a little bit of practice before runners can get the synchronization down. Increase the speed of the runners as they improve their synchronization ability.

Variations: Once the straightaway and curves are mastered add some trickier maneuvers such as: (1) a 180 degree clockwise turn, (2) a 360 degree turn, (3) a clockwise 180 degree turn followed by a 180 degree counter clockwise turn. (4) Coaches can judge which group is the most synchronized, giving them 1-10 ratings, similar to Olympic synchronized diving. (5) Emphasize staying close to each other. If each group keeps the line within a one-meter distance from each other, they receive a point.

Equipment: None needed

Note: Synchronized diving is in the Olympics, so synchronized running may be next! Start practicing; it could be a ticket to be in the Olympic Games.

Cheetahs, Deer, and Elephants

Objective: To simulate running like different animals to experience what the changing speeds of fartlek feels like

Description: Runners spread out over the designated playing area. When the coach calls out "cheetah," the runners sprint and imagine they are a cheetah. When "deer" is called out, the runners run at a fast pace (but not all out), concentrating on good form imagining they are a deer running. When "horse" is called out, the runners will run at an easy pace. When "elephant" is called out, the runners race walk, imagining they are an elephant, swinging their arms powerfully. When "dog" is called out, the runners will jog. When "turtle" is called out, the runners will walk slowly. The coach/leader should call out fast and slow animals to allow for both higher intensity running and recovery. This is an excellent activity for introducing fartlek training where runners can feel the difference between changing speeds.

Variations: (1) Incorporate the use of different animals. (2) To progress to harder workouts, increase the length of time for faster animals. (3) To decrease the recovery time, allow less time for slower animals.

Equipment: None needed

| Cheetahs, Deer, and Elephants ||
Animal	Pace
Cheetah	Sprint
Deer	Fast Pace
Horse	Easy Pace Run
Elephant	Race Walk
Dog	Jog
Turtle	Walk slowly

ETA (Estimated Time of Arrival)

Objective: To estimate how long it would take to perform a list of multiple physical activities.

Description: Divide into three to five runners per group. Each group draws an exercise card with a list of five activities and the location where they will perform the activities. Before beginning, the group gets together and estimates how long it will take the group to complete the five exercise stations at the different locations and get back to the start. The group should run together and each person in the group must complete the exercise at each station before the group can move on. Everyone does the same number of repetitions at each station. The team that gets to a station first has the right of way and the other team must wait until the first team gets started. The team that most accurately predicts their finishing time wins. The order of the team activities on each card should be mixed up to avoid all groups going to the same station at the same time. The team closest to their predicted time wins. Runners are not allowed to wear watches.

Examples of Four Groups:

Group 1	
Station 1	30 Sit-ups at the NE corner of the track
Station 2	One lap around the football stadium
Station 3	2 x 100 meter strides on the football field
Station 4	15 Push- ups at the NW corner of the tennis courts
Station 5	Skip 50 yards starting on the SE corner of the football field

Group 2	
Station 1	One lap around the football stadium
Station 2	2 x 100 meter strides on the football field
Station 3	15 push- ups at the NW corner of the tennis courts
Station 4	Skip 50 yards starting on the SE corner of the football field
Station 5	30 sit-ups at the NE corner of the track

Group 3	
Station 1	2 x 100 meter strides on the football field
Station 2	15 push- ups at the NW corner of the tennis courts
Station 3	Skip 50 yards starting on the SE corner of the football field
Station 4	30 sit-ups at the NE corner of the trail
Station 5	One lap around the football stadium

Group 4	
Station 1	Skip 50 yards starting on the SE corner of the football field
Station 2	30 sit-ups at the NE corner of the track
Station 3	15 push- ups at the NW corner of the tennis courts
Station 4	One lap around the football stadium
Station 5	2 x 100 meter strides on the football field

Variations: (1) Run as individuals. (2) Repeat the activities a number of times and determine the cumulative time off the estimated time.

Equipment: Cards with lists of activities and locations

Visualization Run

Objective: To enjoy visualizing a scenario while running

Description: The coach designates a running area. Each runner will run for a designated time and act out a dream. The coach may provide a list of possible scenarios. While running, the runners act out what the scenario might look like. For example: winning the Olympic Games, setting a 100-meter world record, or beating Usain Bolt. After a designated time period, allow a short recovery period and pick another dream to act out.

Possible visualizations:

- anchoring a winning 4 x 100 relay
- setting a new world record in the 200 meters
- upsetting an Olympic Champion
- winning the state championship
- outsprinting Usain Bolt
- setting a world record in the 100 meters
- anchoring a come-from-behind win in the 4 x 400 relay
- beating the best runners in the world at 400 meter

Variations: The coach may dictate what visualization to act out with all runners acting out the same visualization.

Equipment: None needed

Stride Counter

Objective: To estimate the number of strides it takes to run to destinations

Description: Form groups with eight to 10 runners in each group. Take turns so everyone within the group receives an opportunity to be a leader. The leader picks an object to sprint to approximately 50 to 400 meters away. The exact distance to the object does not need to be known. Before starting the run, each runner in the group predicts how many strides it will take them, individually, to run the designated distance to the object. The runners should count every stride they take as they run to the object. Runners must run in a normal stride length. When all the runners within the group have arrived at the chosen destination, each runner's predicted stride count is compared to his/he actual stride count to compare to his/her estimate. Runners are responsible for counting their own strides. Remind the runners that they are on the honor system!

Variations: (1) Run a measured known distance, such as 100 meters, and count your steps. (2) Run multiple times and tally the total difference at the end to see who was closest to their prediction. (3) Run as a team event with four to five runners in a group and count the total for each team to see which team comes closest to their prediction.

Equipment: Recording sheet

Scoring Golf

Objective: To sprint from tee to green

Description: Find a suitable area and mark your own golf course by laying out cones for the tees and greens. Mark which cones represent tees and greens by using T1 = Tee 1, G1 = Green 1, etc. Make the distance for the greens a sprinting distance. The sprinters will race from the tee to the green. The point scoring system for cross country is used with one point for first, two points for second, etc. Each individual keeps track of his or her points. Walk/jog to the next tee and continue for 9-18 holes.

Variations: (1) Divide into teams and use cumulative team scoring, using cross country scoring. (2) Use individual time and record the times for each hole. Add up all the times at the end. (3) Use team time by adding up all the individual times for each hole.

Equipment: Cones to mark the tees and greens

Speedy Disc Golf

Objective: To sprint over a disc golf course in the shortest time

Description: Find a suitable area and mark your own golf course by laying out cones for the tees and greens. Mark which cones represent tees and greens by using T1 = Tee 1, G1 = Green 1, etc. Divide into groups with three to four runners in each group. Each group should have one disc. Each member of the group should have a throwing order number. The runner throwing first in the rotation throws toward the disc goal. All team members run to where the disc has been thrown. The runner throwing second in the rotation picks the disc up and throws it to the goal. No running with the disc is allowed. Once the disc is in the goal, the entire group runs to the next tee and the next person in the rotation throws. The purpose is not the least number of throws but who can complete the course the fastest. Spread all the teams out at different holes over the course to start. The teams are responsible for timing themselves. The goal is to have the fastest overall time for the designated number of holes.

Variations: (1) Add a stroke element by adding 10 seconds to the time for every throw that is taken. (2) Participate as individuals instead of groups. An individual throws, retrieves, and continues with his or her own disc. You may wish to number the discs to eliminate confusion. To reduce the risk of getting hit by a disk, limit a playing group to four people and spread out groups to start at different holes over the course. (3) Play for a designated time period and see who can complete the most holes. If you complete 18 holes, start over again.

Equipment: Disc for each team, or a disc for each individual if playing individually

Out and Back Pacer

Objective: To run the same pace on a course going out and coming back

Description: Designate a running area with a common start-finish line. Runners are not allowed to wear watches. On command, the runners start sprinting down the field. After a time period determined by the coach, the coach blows the whistle and all runners will stop where they are. The coach notes the running time. After a brief recovery period, the whistle is blown again and runners attempt to run back to the starting point at the exact same pace. The whistle is blown again when the time matches the first run. The runner closest to the start/finish line wins. Give points similar to cross country where the winner gets one point, second place gets two points, etc. Perform the activity for a series of runs 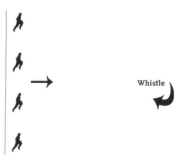 and tally the points. Low score wins! The runners must keep their pace and can't stop or slow as they approach the finish line. Some runners may have to continue running past the finish line.

Variations: (1) If runners slow down as they near the finish line so they don't go over the line, penalize them with a point. (2) Determine a winner by using the distance each runner is from the start/finish line, measured by having the runner count it with steps.

Equipment: Stopwatch, whistle, recording sheet

Hill Tag

 **Objective:** To have fun playing tag and at the same time practice running uphill

Description: This workout works best with a playing field that is uphill such as in a park. The area does not have to be completely open and can contain trees. Form three to four groups with four to 12 runners in each group. Designate a starting line at the bottom of the hill and a goal line at the top of the hill. Also designate the side boundaries. Designate one group to be the taggers first and they will start at the goal line (top of the hill). All of the other runners will start at the starting line (bottom of the hill) and attempt to run to the goal line without being tagged. Runners can avoid being tagged if they take at least three steps downhill (but remember, the goal is to run uphill.) If tagged, the runner runs back to the starting line, by running down the sideline, starts from the starting line again and tries to score. If runners are not tagged before they cross the goal line they score one point and run down the side boundary to return to the starting line and attempt to score again. Each individual keeps track of the points that they score. At the end of the designated time, the runners of each group gather and total their scores. In round two, another group becomes the taggers. Continue the game until each group has had an opportunity to be taggers. Add up the points from each round to determine which group scored the most points.

Variations: (1) Runners must run to the sideline and perform an exercise after being tagged. (2) Runners do not have to go back to the start; they may begin going uphill again after performing an exercise.

Equipment: Cones to mark the boundaries

R-U-N (Running version of Basketball HORSE game)

Objective: To challenge teammates in a running task (similar to a basketball game of HORSE)

Description: Form groups with three or four runners of equal ability in each group. Establish a numerical order in the group. Runner 1 will issue a challenge to the other runners in the group. For example: "Run 100 meters in 16 to 17 seconds." Runner number 1 then takes the challenge and attempts to run 100 meters in 16 to 17 seconds. The other members of the group will time the partner and run behind them. If runner 1 achieves his/her stated goal, the other runners in the group must match the challenge. Runner 1 will time the other runners in the group and run behind them as runner 1 takes the challenge. If the challenge is not met, the other runners receive the letter R. If runner 1 does not achieve what he/she stated, the other runners do not have to attempt to match it and it becomes runner number 2's turn. Runner number 2 is free to do what he/she wants. Runners continue receiving the letters R-U-N. Once a runner receives an N, that runner is out of the game and must help judge or time.

Variations: (1) Limit the group to two people and they time each other. (2) Two people work together to perform the activity and both must achieve the stated standard.

R-U-N Example Activities
Run 100 meters under 14 seconds
Run a 400 meters in 70 to 75 seconds
Run 200 meters in 45 to 46 seconds

Equipment: Each group will need a stopwatch.

Note: This is designed off the game of H-O-R-S-E in basketball.

Move Out and Pick Up

Objective: To work on running the curve and building speed endurance

Description: Sprinters will start in lane one of the track and run counter-clockwise. Sprinters are timed for the 200 meters. The first 200 should be at a slower pace. The sprinters walk/jog 200 meters to recover. After completing the first lap, the sprinter will move out to run in the second lane, but not use the stagger. Running in the second lane will cause the sprinter to run further but the goal is to run it in the same time as the first lap. As the runner continues to move out one lane (and not using staggers) after finishing each interval, the runner will continue to run further and therefore have to run a faster pace. Start the runners at different times to avoid the congestion if they were all to start at the same time. This workout challenges the sprinter to continuously pick up the pace.

Variations: (1) Start in lane 8 and run very fast to begin with. Move in a lane on each interval as the pace becomes progressively slower. (2) Run lanes 1-4 and do repeats. (3) Run lane 1 and skip to lane 5 to practice changing from a slow to a fast pace. (4) There are endless combinations of lane movements.

Equipment: Stopwatch

Sprinter's Pentathlon

Objective: To determine the best all-around sprinter in an event scored decathlon style

Description: Each sprinter will compete in five track races (300 meters-100 meters-200 meters-50 meters-400 meters) with 10-30 minutes recovery time between runs. Points are scored for each sprint based on the running time with the use of a decathlon scoring type chart. With an equal mix of different length sprints, this competition challenges sprinters to determine the best all-around sprinter. Every runner runs the 300 meters. Their time is recorded on the scoring chart. Compare the time to the corresponding score on the scoring tables and record their score in points. Give the runners a certain amount of recovery time (15 minutes for workout, 20-30 minutes if you are using the sprinter's pentathlon as a competition). Start the next event, the 100 meters, and time everyone. Record the time on the scoring chart and record the points off the scoring tables. Keep a running cumulative total. Continue the event by running 200 meters-50 meters-400 meters. After the last event, complete the event by announcing the point totals.

Variations: (1) Use a long version of the Sprinter's Pentathlon by running 400-100-50-200-800.

Equipment: Scoring chart, scoring tables, stopwatches.

Short Version Scoring Table

Points	300 meters	100 meters	200 meters	50 meters	400 meters
700	31.17	9.90	19.78	5.80	44.45
690	31.56	10.01	20.02	5.86	44.99
680	31.96	10.11	20.26	5.92	45.54
670	32.36	10.22	20.5	5.98	46.09
660	32.76	10.33	20.74	6.04	46.64
650	33.16	10.43	20.99	6.10	47.20
640	33.57	10.54	21.23	6.16	47.76
630	33.98	10.65	21.48	6.22	48.33
620	34.4	10.76	21.73	6.28	48.90
610	34.81	10.87	21.99	6.34	49.48
600	35.24	10.99	22.24	6.40	50.06
590	35.66	11.10	22.5	6.47	50.64
580	36.09	11.21	22.76	6.53	51.23
570	36.52	11.33	23.02	6.59	51.83
560	36.00	11.44	23.29	6.65	52.43
550	37.40	11.56	23.55	6.71	53.04
540	37.84	11.68	23.82	6.76	53.65
530	38.29	11.80	24.09	6.83	54.26
520	38.74	11.92	24.37	6.89	54.89
510	39.20	12.04	24.64	6.95	55.52
500	39.66	12.16	24.92	7.01	56.15
490	40.12	12.29	25.20	7.07	56.79
480	40.60	12.41	25.49	7.13	57.44
470	41.07	12.54	25.78	7.19	58.10

Points	300 meters	100 meters	200 meters	50 meters	400 meters
460	41.55	12.67	26.07	7.25	58.76
450	42.04	12.80	26.36	7.31	59.43
440	42.53	12.93	26.66	7.37	1:00.10
430	43.03	13.06	26.96	7.43	1:00.79
420	43.53	13.19	27.27	7.49	1:01.48
410	44.04	13.33	27.57	7.55	1:02.18
400	44.55	13.47	27.89	7.61	1:02.89
390	45.07	13.61	28.20	7.67	1:03.61
380	45.60	13.75	28.52	7.74	1:04.34
370	46.14	13.89	28.85	7.80	1:05.08
360	46.68	14.03	29.18	7.86	1:05.82
350	47.23	14.18	29.51	7.92	1:06.58
340	47.79	14.33	29.85	7.98	1:07.35
330	48.35	14.48	30.19	8.04	1:08.13
320	48.93	14.63	30.54	8.10	1:08.92
310	49.51	14.79	30.89	8.16	1:09.73
300	50.10	14.94	31.25	8.22	1:10.54
290	50.71	15.11	31.62	8.31	1:11.37
280	51.32	15.27	31.99	8.37	1:12.22
270	51.95	15.43	32.37	8.43	1:13.08
260	52.58	15.60	32.75	8.49	1:13.96
250	53.23	15.78	33.15	8.55	1:14.85
240	53.89	15.95	33.55	8.64	1:15.76
230	54.57	16.13	33.96	8.70	1:16.70
220	55.26	16.32	34.38	8.76	1:17.65
210	55.97	16.51	34.80	8.82	1:18.62
200	56.69	16.70	35.24	8.88	1:19.62
190	57.43	16.90	35.69	8.94	1:20.64
180	58.20	17.10	36.15	9.00	1:21.69
170	58.98	17.31	36.63	9.06	1:22.77
160	59.79	17.52	37.12	9.12	1:23.88
150	60.62	17.74	37.62	9.18	1:25.03
140	61.48	17.97	38.14	9.24	1:26.21
130	62.37	18.21	38.68	9.30	1:27.44
120	63.30	18.46	39.25	9.36	1:28.72
110	64.26	18.71	39.83	9.42	1:30.05
100	65.28	18.98	40.44	9.48	1:31.45
90	66.34	19.27	41.09	9.54	1:32.91
80	67.46	19.57	41.77	9.60	1:34.46
70	68.66	19.88	42.49	9.67	1:36.11
60	69.95	20.23	43.27	9.73	1:37.88
50	71.35	20.60	44.12	9.79	1:39.81
40	72.89	21.01	45.06	9.84	1:41.94
30	74.65	21.48	46.12	9.90	1:44.36
20	76.73	22.03	47.38	9.96	1:47.23
10	79.45	22.76	49.03	10.02	1:50.97

Long Version Scoring Table

Points	400 meters	100 meters	50 meters	200 meters	800 meters
700	44.45	9.90	5.80	19.78	1:46.80
690	44.99	10.01	5.86	20.02	1:47.80
680	45.54	10.11	5.92	20.26	1:48.90
670	46.09	10.22	5.98	20.50	1:49.90
660	46.64	10.33	6.04	20.74	1:50.90
650	47.20	10.43	6.10	20.99	1:52.00
640	47.76	10.54	6.16	21.23	1:53.10
630	48.33	10.65	6.22	21.48	1:54.10
620	48.90	10.76	6.28	21.73	1:55.20
610	49.48	10.87	6.34	21.99	1:56.30
600	50.06	10.99	6.40	22.24	1:57.40
590	50.64	11.10	6.47	22.50	1:58.50
580	51.23	11.21	6.53	22.76	1:59.60
570	51.83	11.33	6.59	23.02	2:00.80
560	52.43	11.44	6.65	23.29	2:01.90
550	53.04	11.56	6.71	23.55	2:03.10
540	53.65	11.68	6.76	23.82	2:04.20
530	54.26	11.80	6.83	24.09	2:05.40
520	54.89	11.92	6.89	24.37	2:06.60
510	55.52	12.04	6.95	24.64	2:07.80
500	56.15	12.16	7.01	24.92	2:09.00
490	56.79	12.29	7.07	25.20	2:10.20
480	57.44	12.41	7.13	25.49	2:11.40
470	58.10	12.54	7.19	25.78	2:12.00
460	58.76	12.67	7.25	26.07	2:13.90
450	59.43	12.80	7.31	26.36	2:15.20
440	1:00.1	12.93	7.37	26.66	2:16.60
430	1:00.8	13.06	7.43	26.96	2:17.80
420	1:01.5	13.19	7.49	27.27	2:19.10
410	1:02.2	13.33	7.55	27.57	2:20.40
400	1:02.9	13.47	7.61	27.89	2:21.00
390	1:03.6	13.61	7.67	28.20	2:23.10
380	1:04.3	13.75	7.74	28.52	2:24.50
370	1:05.1	13.89	7.80	28.85	2:25.90
360	1:05.8	14.03	7.86	29.18	2:27.30
350	1:06.6	14.18	7.92	29.51	2:28.70
340	1:07.4	14.33	7.98	29.85	2:30.20
330	1:08.1	14.48	8.04	30.19	2:31.70
320	1:08.9	14.63	8.10	30.54	2:33.20
310	1:09.7	14.79	8.16	30.89	2:34.70

Points	400 meters	100 meters	50 meters	200 meters	800 meters
300	1:10.5	14.94	8.22	31.25	2:36.30
290	1:11.4	15.11	8.31	31.62	2:37.80
280	1:12.2	15.27	8.37	31.99	2:39.40
270	1:13.1	15.43	8.43	32.37	2:41.10
260	1:14.0	15.60	8.49	32.75	2:42.70
250	1:14.8	15.78	8.55	33.15	2:44.40
240	1:15.8	15.95	8.64	33.55	2:46.20
230	1:16.7	16.13	8.70	33.96	2:47.90
220	1:17.6	16.32	8.76	34.38	2:49.70
210	1:18.6	16.51	8.82	34.80	2:51.60
200	1:19.6	16.70	8.88	35.24	2:53.50
190	1:20.6	16.90	8.94	35.69	2:55.40
180	1:21.7	17.10	9.00	36.15	2:57.40
170	1:22.8	17.31	9.06	36.63	2:59.40
160	1:23.9	17.52	9.12	37.12	3:01.50
150	1:25.0	17.74	9.18	37.62	3:03.70
140	1:26.2	17.97	9.24	38.14	3:06.00
130	1:27.4	18.21	9.30	38.68	3:08.30
120	1:28.7	18.46	9.36	39.25	3:10.70
110	1:30.1	18.71	9.42	39.83	3:13.20
100	1:31.5	18.98	9.48	40.44	3:15.90
90	1:32.9	19.27	9.54	41.09	3:18.60
80	1:34.5	19.57	9.60	41.77	3:21.60
70	1:36.1	19.88	9.67	42.49	3:24.70
60	1:37.9	20.23	9.73	43.27	3:28.10
50	1:39.8	20.60	9.79	44.12	3:31.70
40	1:41.9	21.01	9.84	45.06	3:35.80
30	1:44.4	21.48	9.90	46.12	3:40.30
20	1:47.2	22.03	9.96	47.38	3:45.80
10	1:51.0	22.76	10.02	49.03	3:52.90

Chapter 13 - Hurdles

Hurdling is the act of running and clearing barriers with speed. Track and field hurdle events have a long history. In the early 1800s, hurdle races of 100 yards were run over heavy wooden barriers. The distance was extended to 110 meters in 1888. The longer 400-meter hurdle race was introduced in 1860. Runners jumped over 12 heavy wooden barriers (that did not move when hit) that were spaced equal distances apart. The 110-meter hurdles were introduced as an Olympic Games race in 1896, just after the heavy, solid hurdles were replaced with lighter-weight hurdles that could be knocked over forwards. The 400-meter hurdles became an Olympic sport for men in 1900. The first women's hurdle races were run in 1926 over a distance of 80 meters. The event attained Olympic status in 1932. In 1969, the distance was extended to 100 meters, which became the standard at the Olympics beginning in 1972. Women didn't run the 400 meter hurdles at the Olympics until 1984.

The standard sprint or short hurdle race is 110 meters for men and 100 meters for women; however, indoor races, youth and masters races are run at different distances. The standard long hurdle race is 400 meters for both men and women. Each of these races is run over 10 hurdles and they are all Olympic events. Many groups run 300-meter hurdles and youth run 200-meter hurdles.

Speed is an important component of the hurdles. Athletes should be taught to run (sprint) over the hurdles instead of jumping over them. The games presented in this chapter have an objective of developing the technique with well-planned steps leading up to and between each hurdle. Generally, the efficient hurdler spends the minimum amount of time and energy going vertically over the hurdle, thus achieving maximum speed in the horizontal race direction down the track. In the 100 and 110-meter hurdle events, the fastest hurdlers use the three-step technique between hurdles. Younger hurdlers should focus on the speed and rhythm of going over hurdles and many of the games use lower hurdles and different spacing between hurdles that allow the hurdler to develop speed and rhythm.

Safety in track and field is always a priority. Care should be taken that the hurdles are in good working order with no sharp edges and the top bar being secure. In many of the games, improvised equipment is used. Ensure that the equipment used is safe. Hurdles should never be crossed in the wrong direction (i.e. from the landing side) with the counter-balance weights also relatively correctly positioned. Track and field coaches should always consult their specific rule book and follow the important information regarding equipment specifications and safety.

Athlete Hurdle Relay

Objective: To practice hurdling skills by jumping over teammates

Description: Form teams of four to six athletes. Each team member lies down parallel to each other, five yards apart. On command, the first athlete in line stands up and proceeds to hurdle over each athlete lying down. When the athlete gets to the end of the line, he/she lies down five yards from the last athlete and the next athlete at the front of the line starts and hurdles over everyone in line. Continue until the line has progressed to the end of the designated playing area.

Variations: Run as a race with teams competing against each other.

Equipment: Soft surface, cones to mark the start and end of area

Nature Hurdles

Objective: To have fun for beginning hurdlers

Description: Form groups of four athletes spread out over the designated playing area. One athlcte in each group adopts one of the following roles: runner, stone (crouched down), a bridge (standing legs wide apart) and a tree (standing hands raised). On command, the runner runs and jumps over the stone, crawls under the bridge and hops around the tree and returns to take the place of the stone, who assumes the role of the runner and performs all three activities and then replaces the bridge, the bridge becomes the runner and performs all three activities and then replaces the tree. Once the tree finishes, one cycle has been completed. This is a good warm-up activity.

Variations: (1) Increase the distance between the stone, bridge and the tree. (2) Change the mode of hurdling (different lead legs) over the stone and jumping (right leg, left leg) around the tree.

Equipment: None needed

Bricks and Sticks

Objective: To introduce beginners to the hurdles

Description: This activity can be used as an introductory drill before attempting to use real, full sized hurdles. It is based upon the bricks and sticks approach of allowing the athletes to hurdle over a low height and gradually increase the height of the hurdle. The use of a broomstick or pool noodle balanced on blocks allows the athlete to gradually increase the height by progressing to multiple wooden blocks. Spread out the jumping obstacles so that there is plenty of room to hurdle.

Variations: (1) Start with one hurdle and emphasize good form. (2) When the athlete becomes comfortable with running over the "bricks and sticks," add multiple barriers. (3) Increase the distance between hurdles.

Equipment: Cones, crossbars

Pizza Box Hurdle

Objectives: To learn beginning hurdling skills and develop a rhythmic pattern

Description: Beginning hurdlers often think the hurdles are a jumping event and slow down and jump too high vertically over the obstacle. This activity allows the beginning athlete to run over an obstacle that is low to the ground and maintain sprint form. Set pizza boxes on the ground about five meters apart. Have athletes run one at a time and sprint over the pizza boxes.

Variations: (1) Time the athletes over the boxes and encourage them to sprint. (2) Add pizza boxes on top of each other to make a higher hurdle height. (3) Jump over an actual pizza and eat it when done (hopefully nobody steps on it). (4) Order a pizza!

Equipment: Pizza box

Kangaroo Relay

Objective: To practice hurdling technique

Description: Two athletes will hold the ends of a pool noodle with their partner. Other groups of two will also hold pool noodles and be spread out approximately 10 meters from each other. The noodle is kept about 12 inches (30 centimeters) off the ground. Two athletes will be designated as the hurdlers and go one at a time moving down the line of teammates hurdling each team member's noodle. When the first two athletes are done hurdling, they become the first two athletes in line holding the noodle. All groups move down 10 meters and the last two partners will become the new hurdlers.

Variations: (1) Raise or lower heights that the noodles are held. (2) Increase the distance between hurdles.

Equipment: Pool noodles

Bean Bag Hurdling

Objective: To practice the hurdling skill

Description: Form teams of equal numbers. With cones, mark a square playing area. The teams line up in the corners of the playing area. Set up a low beginner hurdle (cones and a crossbar) evenly spaced from the corner of the square to the center of the square. A hula hoop is placed behind each team line at the corners. In the center of the square, place several bean bags in a hula hoop. The first athlete in line will run over the hurdle to the center, grab a bean bag and hurdle

123

back to the team line, where the bean bag is placed inside the hoop. Once the bean bag has been placed in the hoop the next runner goes. The team with the most bean bags after a designated time is the winner.

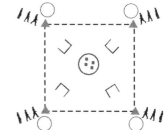

Variations: (1) Every other athlete will return the bean bags to the center. (2) Add a second hurdle spaced evenly apart. (3) Add a third hurdle.

Equipment: Cones to mark the corners, bean bags, hula hoops

Hurdle Mobility

Objectives: To improve flexibility and power

Description: Set up four to seven hurdles in a line so that barriers are parallel and are butted against each other. The hurdles should be set at a height that allows athletes to stand astride the hurdle while standing on their toes. If there are more than eight athletes, set up another station to minimize waiting in line. Athletes should maintain a tucked hip position and move the arms in conjunction with the legs. Athletes should step over each hurdle and touch both feet between each hurdle.

Variations: Try the following: (1) lead with left then right, (2) walkover-only one foot lands between each, (3) backward walkovers, (4) step-overs, (5) sideways step, (6) over-under (focus on hip flexors), (7) hold hands overhead or behind the head for advanced balance training, (8) hold a medicine ball.

Equipment: Hurdles

Hurdle Walkover Lead Leg

Objective: To work on lead leg action

Description: Set up low hurdles for the athlete to walk beside. If the athlete's leading leg is the right, he/she walks on the left side of the hurdle. The opposite is required if his/her leading leg is the left. The athlete drives the thigh up and extends it over the low hurdle, then drives it forward and touches the ground. When the athlete is finished, he/she walks to the next hurdle and repeats the process. This drill does not require the trailing leg to do anything. The emphasis is on driving up with the leading leg. Make sure a hurdle height is selected that is low enough to do this. Lift the lead leg straight up, not to the side and keep it flexed when doing so.

Variations: (1) Once the athlete becomes familiar with the drill, see how many times the athlete can do the drill in 15 seconds. (3) In 30 seconds. (4) The athletes challenges their partners to see who can get the most in a designated time.

Equipment: Hurdles, stopwatch

Hurdle Walkover Trail Leg

Objective: To work on lead leg action

Description: Each athlete will need a partner for this drill. One hurdler stands to the side of a low hurdle. If the trailing leg is the left, the athlete stands on the right side of the hurdle. The opposite will be for right trailing legs. The athlete stands on his/her leading leg and brings the trailing leg over across the hurdle. Before doing so, the athlete leans forward and grabs ahold of his/her partner for balance. This simulates the forward body lean during a race. The athlete slowly brings the trailing leg over the hurdle and then down to the ground. Repeat several times slowly and then increase speed. Switch partners. The emphasis here is on getting the trailing leg to clear the bar and do so quickly. However, emphasize starting slowly and giving athletes time to develop this skill.

Variations: (1) Once the athlete becomes familiar with the drill, see how many times the athlete can pull the trail leg through in 15 seconds. (2) In 30 seconds. (3) The athlete challenges his/her partner to see who can get the most in a designated time.

Equipment: Hurdles, stopwatch

Hurdle Spacing Racing

Objectives: To work on acceleration and maximum velocity

Description: Low barriers or hurdles are spaced closer together than normal. Moving the hurdles closer together and keeping the barriers low allows athletes to rhythmically complete repetitions without stutter-stepping or reaching for the hurdles. The athletes will use their feet to measure how far from the hurdle marking on the track the hurdles will be positioned. Start off with the first hurdle moved in three feet, the second needs to be moved in six feet, and so on. Keep the barriers low.

Variations: Once the athlete develops a rhythm in the hurdles, gradually increase (1) the height of the hurdle and (2) the distance between hurdles.

Equipment: Barriers, hurdles

Mirror Hurdles

Objective: To develop a step pattern in the hurdles

Description: Each athlete will need a partner. Set two hurdles six meters apart. In a lane without the hurdles, the athlete mimics the hurdling action. The athlete attempts to take only three strides between hurdles. The partner marks where the athlete took off and landed from. After both athletes have practiced in the lane without hurdles, run in the lane with the hurdles and run over the two hurdles. Measure the take-off and landing distance from the hurdle and compare to the non-hurdle markings. The goal is to only use three strides between hurdles. If the athlete can successfully do this three times at a distance of six meters, spread the hurdles out to seven meters. If this is completed three times then spread the hurdles out to eight meters. Compare the take-off and landing distance from the hurdle at each distance.

Variations: Increase the number of hurdles

Equipment: Hurdles, chalk

Shuttle Hurdle-Sprint Relay

Objective: To run a shuttle relay of combined sprint and hurdle distances

Description: Two lanes are necessary for each team: one lane with four hurdles set at a low height and six meters apart and the other lane without hurdles. Form two teams and line up in single file line with half of the team on the starting line and the other half of the team on the end of the running lane. The first athlete will run the hurdle lane and touch hands with the teammate waiting at the end line. The second athlete on the team runs the sprint lane back to the next teammate who hurdles. The event is completed once each team member has run both sprint and hurdle distances.

Variations: (1) Each athlete hurdles down, turns around, and sprints back before the next teammate goes. (2) Run individually with the best time the winner. (3) Run three times and take the best time. (4) Increase the distance between hurdles.

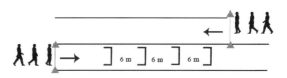

Equipment: Hurdles, cones

Shuttle Hurdle Relay

Objective: To sprint over hurdles at regular intervals

Description: Form teams of four runners, with two of them forming a single file line on one end and the other two forming a single file line at the opposite end facing the other runners and in an adjacent lane. Start with the hurdles six meters apart. On command, the first runner sprints and hurdles to the opposite end. When the first runner crosses the finish line, the second runner can start running hurdles in the opposite direction. Continue until all runners have run. Since each team occupies two side by side lanes, there are a maximum of only four teams in any one heat for an eight-lane track. There is no baton used in this race.

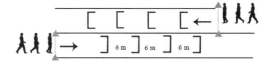

Variations: (1) Run different numbers of hurdles. (2) Increase the distance between hurdles.

Equipment: Hurdles

Obstacle Course Hurdling

Objective: To work on hurdling over different obstacles and using different step patterns

Description: Develop a loop course with a total distance of approximately 100 meters long. One area will be the sprint area, one area will be designed for sprinting over hurdles and one area will be designed as a slalom course to sprint around. Run as a relay with the athletes touching hands instead of using a baton. Play for a designated number of loops or time.

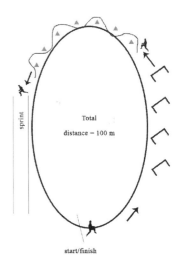

Variations: (1) Run as individuals, timing each runner. (2) Run as a relay so that when a teammate clears the first obstacle in the loop, the next runner may start.

Equipment: Low obstacles to jump over, low hurdles, cones for slalom

Dice Hurdling

Objective: To determine the number of hurdles to run based upon the roll of dice

Description: Roll one die to see how many hurdles the hurdler will run at one time. After the hurdler runs, he/she returns to roll the die again to determine the next hurdle run.

Variations: (1) Add up the total for both dice to determine the number of seconds the athlete sprints. Roll both dice and do an anaerobic workout by sprinting the number of seconds on the dice. (2) Read the low die first. A one and three would be 13 seconds running time. (3) Use the high die first. If a one and three were rolled on the dice, that would mean a 31 second run.

Equipment: Dice, hurdles

Dice Hurdling Example				
Overall Running Time Desired: 30-35 minutes				
	Die 1	Die 2	Seconds Run	Cumulative Time
Roll 1	5	4	9	9
Roll 2	2	3	5	14
Roll 3	1	4	5	19
Roll 4	4	6	10	29
Roll 5	2	3	5	34

Partner Pacer

Objective: To develop stamina, speed endurance and tempo

Description: Each hurdler will need a partner. Using a combination of hurdles and running on the flat will help increase the hurdler's performance level. While one partner is hurdling, the other is running on the flat. Partners can help each other out by pacing. One partner will run a 400 meter, with 200 meters on the flat and the last 200 meters over hurdles. At the same time, the other partner will run 200 meters over five hurdles and then 200 meters on the flat. On the second set of intervals, the order of hurdling and running on the flat is reversed.

Variations: Change the distances (i.e. Partner 1 runs 300 meters over hurdles and 100 flat while partner 2 runs 300 flat and 100 hurdles)

Equipment: Hurdles

Chapter 14 - Distance

The ancient history of running goes back to humans hunting animals for food to survive. The runner would run at a slow and steady pace sometimes for days. The animal, running in spurts, had to stop in order to cool itself, and eventually would collapse from exhaustion and heat. With developments in agriculture and culture, long distance running developed many purposes other than hunting such as religious ceremonies, delivering messages for military and political purposes, and sport.

The history of long-distance track running events evolved in the track and field stadiums where they are held. Oval circuits allow athletes to cover long distances in a confined area. The early tracks were on marked areas of dirt or grass. Running tracks became more refined during the 20th century when oval running tracks were standardized to 400 meters in distance and cinder tracks were replaced by synthetic all-weather running tracks starting in the mid-1960s.

The distance games in this chapter can be incorporated into a running program to allow runners to not only develop physically and mentally, but to also enhance the enjoyment of running longer distances. Many runners, especially beginners, prefer running shorter distances and may not enjoy the long runs. This could be because of lack of endurance, as the longer one runs the more uncomfortable it becomes when one is not in shape. As runners properly prepare, physiological and psychological adaptations occur and the long run become more comfortable and enjoyable.

Safety in track and field is always a priority. Proper progression in terms of volume and intensity are important in monitoring the development of the distance runner. When running off the track, careful planning and communication to athletes on defining boundaries for distance running and safety rules are invaluable in making the run safe and enjoyable.

Flying Geese

 Objective: To run together in a V formation, like geese flying to achieve a common goal

Description: If possible, form groups of seven or nine runners. Each group of runners will run in a V formation like flying geese. After a designated time period of running, the front runner drops to the back on the right side of the formation. The next runner on the left side of the formation will move to the lead. After a designated time period, the new lead runner drops to the back on the left side and the next person on the left side of the line moves up. Continue alternating leaders on the right and left side moving up until everyone has had an opportunity to lead.

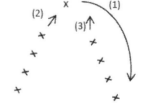

Variations: (1) The coach blows the whistle for front runners to drop to the back of the formation. (2) Run the flying geese formation as a fast fartlek workout.

Progressive Endurance

Objective: To work on endurance by running at a progressive speed

Description: Form teams of four to 10 athletes per team. Each team member starts at the start/finish line and has to run a course of 100 meters as often as possible at a progressive pace. Determine a slow jogging pace that athletes will run the first lap in. The coach will time the lap and blow the whistle at the pace time. Each athlete that crosses the finish line before the whistle blows receives a point for his/her team. Each lap will get two seconds faster. This is a continuous run. If a runner does not make the time, that runner continues to run but does not score a point for the team that lap. He/she is eligible to score in following laps.

Variations: (1) Vary the course length. (2) Vary the time depending upon the ability level. (3) Decrease the time by more than two seconds per lap.

Equipment: Stopwatch, cones to mark the course

Lap 1: 30 seconds	Lap 7: 18 seconds
Lap 2: 28 seconds	Lap 8: 16 seconds
Lap 3: 26 seconds	Lap 9: 14 seconds
Lap 4: 24 seconds	Lap 10: 12 seconds
Lap 5: 22 seconds	Lap 11: 10 seconds
Lap 6: 20 seconds	

Pace Circle

Objective: To practice pacing

Description: Set up three circles inside each other, with the largest about 200 meters in circumference. Set up three cones side by side on each circle. This can also be done in lanes 1, 4, and 7 on a track. On signal, three runners, one at each circle, begin running and stay even with each other the entire way around. In order to stay even with each other, the outer runners will have to run a faster pace. Rotate from the inside to the outside after each run so everyone has a chance to run the different circles to practice pacing.

Variations: (1) Run more than three runners at a time. (2) Increase the distance of the circles. (3) Add more circles. (4) Allow the inside runners to set the pace.

Equipment: Cones, stopwatch

Tandem Running

Objective: To work with a partner in passing people and running in traffic

Description: Form groups of two runners with equal ability. All groups will run a designated distance. The goal is to have your group be the first to finish. The two partners will run one right behind the other for the entire run. This is similar to two people riding a tandem bike. They must stay within two meters of each other. If the distance becomes more than two meters, they are considered to have crashed their bike and they receive a warning. On the third warning they must start the run over. The coach should use his/her judgment on infractions. The partners may switch leading.

Variations: (1) Instead of running one behind another, athletes must run side by side the entire way. When they pass people, they still must be side by side. (2) Require that after every 30 seconds athletes must switch leading with their partner.

Russian Tag

Objective: Fun speed play that develops teamwork and both the aerobic and anaerobic systems in a fun tag game

Description: Form two single file lines. Each runner should be approximately one arm's length behind the runner in front of them. One runner is designated as the tagger and stands five feet behind the last two runners in the double line. Both lines start running at the same time and run together, maintaining a double line. The taggers run five feet behind the lines. When the taggers shout "Go," the last runner in each line moves to the outside of his/her line and sprints to the front of the line. The taggers can choose going to one side or the other and attempts to tag either runner before they get to the front of the lines. Once the two runners meet at the front of the line and touch palms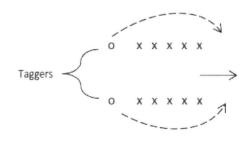
together, they are safe. If the pair is successful in getting to the front of the line and touching palms, the tagger returns to the back of the line to try again. If the taggers are successful in making the tag, the tagged player becomes a new tagger. If the taggers are unsuccessful after three attempts, replace the taggers.

Variations: (1) On the command "Go," the runners being chased move up on the outside of the lines. The tagger runs between the two lines formed by the groups. The objective for the tagger is to high five (tag) a front person in line before the two runners being chased can tag one of the front runners in the line.

Equipment: None needed

Digital Scavenger Hunt

 Objective: To find items on a scavenger hunt by taking digital pictures.

Description: Form groups with four to six runners in each group. Designate the running boundaries. The runners in each group must stay together on the run. Each group has a digital camera or a cell phone camera and a list of things to photograph. Designate a certain time period for groups to take all the pictures on the list and get back. Each team member must take at least one of the pictures. When the runners return, the coach will check to verify that all the items have been photographed. The team that returns first with all the correct items is the winner. If a team does not have all the items, it continues the activity until it has returned with all the items. Place a time limit on the hunt. If the teams have not found all the items, the team with the most items is the winner.

Sample list of items to take pictures of:
Sign with letter "r" in it
Black Dog
Sign that says name of the town
Pine cone
Cow
Tractor (not a riding lawnmower)
Person riding a bike
Two birds in the same picture
Flowers in bloom
Sprinkler watering yard or water running out of hose

Variations: (1) Group members with the exception of the photographer must be in the picture. (2) Add more difficult items to the list and remove the requirement the runners have to stay together. The group will need multiple cameras for this.

Equipment: One digital camera or cell phone for each team and a list of requirements to fulfill.

Shutter Spot

Objective: To run to a location and take a picture with a group and challenge other groups to guess the spot the picture was taken

Description: Form groups with four to six runners in each group. Designate the running boundaries. The runners in each group must stay together on the run. Each group has a digital camera or a cell phone camera. Designate a certain time period for groups to take pictures on the list and get back. Each team member must take at least one of the pictures. On the run, the group will take five to 10 photographs. At the end of time period, all groups will come together and look at each group's photographs. The challenge is to guess the spot that the photograph was taken.

Variations: Narrow down the number of photos to share with other groups from one to three.

Equipment: Digital camera for each group and paper to write down answers for guesses

Can I Make A Copy?

 Objective: To run to a spot, take a picture and challenge other runners to guess where the picture was taken and run to that spot and make a "copy"

Description: Form groups with four to six runners in each group. Designate the running boundaries. The runners in each group must stay together on the run. Each group has a digital camera or a cell phone camera. Designate a certain time period for groups to take pictures on the list and get back.

On the run the group will take one group photograph and return. At the end of time period, all groups will come together and look at the photographs from every team. The challenge will be for each group to guess where the exact spot that the photograph was taken and then run to that spot and take a picture exactly like the original (make a copy) taken by the other groups. For example, if there are five groups, that means that each group will have to run to the other four spots and take a picture. On command, the groups are off to "make a copy." Place a time period for the copy process to be accomplished. All groups return and compare their copy to the original photo.

Variation: (1) In the copy process part of the game, each group will only go to one spot to "make a copy," the coach can select who goes where or the groups can. (2) Number the groups and randomly draw to determine which spot they go to "make a copy."

Equipment: Digital camera for each group

Clue Run

Objective: To receive clues at different running stations that will lead to the final destination

Description: Develop a running course and place clues at each station. Form groups with four to six runners in each group. The runners in each group must stay together on the run. The groups will be provided with an initial clue that will lead them to the first station. At the first station will be a clue that leads them to the next station. Runners continue running to each stations and finding a clue and searching for the next station. Eventually, the runners will end up at the ultimate destination.

Clues that can be given that take advantage of locations on your school grounds:	
Clue	**Destination**
Going high, going low, Hanging still when no one's there, Go with the flow, Back and forth as the wind blows your hair.	Swings on the playground
Shoot for the sky, but not too high 10 feet tall, ball and all.	Basketball goal
Back to nature where the weeds are high, At the head, look down, not towards the sky.	Head of nature trail
Hit a double, don't have to slide, On the ground, you'd tear your hide.	Softball field

Variations: (1) Perform as an individual activity. (2) If the groups are having a difficult time of figuring out the clue, give them some hints.

Equipment: Clues placed at each one of the stations.

Note: I suggest making the clues on a piece of paper. Staple the copies of the clues for each station together and place in a container such as a Ziploc bag or coffee can. Place the clue container where it's visible. Emphasize that runners make take only one clue paper.

Distance Bingo

Objective: While completing a distance run, fill out a bingo distance running card.

Description: Divide into groups of four to six runners in each group. Each group will have one bingo distance card. As the group is running and see something on their bingo card, the athletes mark it off. When the group gets a BINGO, the athletes return and draw another bingo card. Play for a designated time period.

Variations: (1) Complete the Bingo cards as individuals. (2) Use different variations of Bingo such as horizontal, vertical, or diagonal.

Equipment: Bingo cards, sticky dots (peel off adhesive backing) to mark bingo cards

Running Bingo Card 1

Pine Tree	White Fence	FREE	Waterfall	Roses
Cross Walk Sign	Circle Driveway	Brick House	American Flag	Tractor
Gas Station	Cat	Newspaper	Trash Can	Two People Walking Together
White Dog	Red Car	Ball	Black Pick-up	Trailer
Speed Limit Sign	Kids Swing Set	House With 3 Car Garage	Woman Walking	Person Riding a Bike

Running Bingo Card 2

Man Walking	Chain Link Fence	Newspaper	Baby Stroller	Yield Sign
Cross Walk Sign	Circle Driveway	Yellow House	Kansas Flag	Lawnmower
Gas Station	Cat	FREE	Black Dog	Two People Walking Together
Dumpster	Blue Car	Person Riding a Motorcycle	White Pick-up	Trailer
Speed Limit Sign	Kids Swing Set	House With 3 Car Garage	Oak Tree	Ball

Oak Tree	White Fence	Speed Limit Sign	Lawnmower	Black Dog
Cross Walk Sign	Blue Car	Brick House	American Flag	Tractor
Two People Walking Together	Cat	Newspaper	Trash Can	Gas Station
White Dog	Red Car	Ball	Black Pick-up	Trailer
FREE	Kids Swing Set	White Pick-up	Man Walking	Person Riding a Motorcycle

Lap Elimination

Objective: To stay in the game by avoiding being the last person at the end of each lap

Description: Set up a loop course (preferably 200-300 meters). Form groups of four to eight runners of equal ability in each group. All runners in a group start together from a common start-finish line. At the end of the first loop, the last runner to cross the finish line is eliminated from the game. Once a runner is out of the game, he/she must continue running but in the opposite direction around the outside of the loop. The rest of the runners continue running (no stopping). At the end of the second lap, the runner who is last is eliminated. The game continues until all are eliminated except one runner. Smart runners will use strategy. If a runner is a good kicker, he/she will conserve energy and kick at the end. Non-kickers will have to move earlier in the lap to ensure they will not be last person at the end of the lap and be eliminated.

Variations: (1) Once a runner has been eliminated, he/she can run one lap around the outside of the loop and get back in the game. (3) When only one runner is left, hc/shc can run one final victory lap alone.

Equipment: None needed

Primo Run

Objective: To work on getting out fast in a race

Description: Form groups of equal ability. Each group will run a four-lap race. The laps can be of 100 meters, 200 meters, or 400 meters. The leaders at the ¼ mark of the run receives four points for the leader, three points for 2nd place, two points for 3rd place, one for 4th place. The leaders at the ½ mark of the run receive four points for the leader, three points for 2nd place, two points for 3rd place, one point for 4th place. The leaders at the ¾ mark of the run receive four points for the leader, three points for 2nd place, two points for 3rd place, one point for 4th place. Points are doubled at the finish with the winner receiving eight points, six points for 2nd place, four point for 3rd place, two points for 4th place.

Note: In the 5000 meters at the world class DN Galan meet in Stockholm, Sweden, they gave prize money to who was leading at four laps to go, three to go, two to go and one lap go. With a small pack entering the last 1600 together, the racing became crazy, as runners would sprint for the bonus. Sammy Kipketer finished 2nd overall but won more money than the winner because he kept winning the lap bonus.

Variations: (1) Run different distances. (2) Vary the number of bonus points. (3) Give bonus points to only the leader at each point.

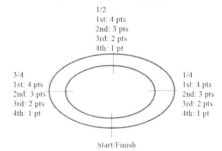

Equipment: Stopwatch

Make It - Take It Intervals

Objective: To lead an interval group and achieve the designated pace time to keep on leading the intervals

Description: Form groups of four to six runners of equal ability in each group. The coach designates a certain time the group should hit for the interval workout. Runner 1 leads the first interval. If Runner 1 is within + or – half a second of the assigned interval time (make it) he/she remains the leader (take it) for the next interval. Runner 1 will continue being the leader until the designated time is not met. When Runner 1 does not make the designated time, a new leader will take over. Continue until you have run the desired number of intervals.

Variation: Score the intervals; each time the runner makes the time, they receive one point.

Equipment: Stopwatch

Running Tournament (Track Madness)

Objective: To run an interval workout and work on pace in a fun manner

Description: Form groups of up to eight runners. Set up a tournament bracket. Each of the eight runners in a group will draw to see where the runner goes in the bracket. Instead of a winners and losers bracket, call it an advance and retreat bracket. Once the runner's name has been placed in the bracket, each runner should determine or be given a pace to hit. The pace should be individualized for each runner and does not have to be the same pace for everyone in the group. The two runners on the same side of the bracket will run against each other and the one closest to their correct pace advances on to the next round. Determine the distance to be run and what the recovery interval will be. The coach reads the time as the runners cross the finish line. Runners should be warned not to adjust their pace if they hear the time before they cross the finish line. Runners determine how far off they were on their pace and go over to the tournament bracket and write their time down by their name in the bracket. After both runners that ran against each other have recorded their times, determine who advances or retreats in the bracket. Everyone runs three rounds to determine the champion and the final places. After a recovery period, redraw positions for a new bracket and a new set of intervals.

Variations: Instead of pace, go off of whoever runs the fastest. You may want to seed the tournament instead of drawing by lot. Encourage the runners to pace themselves, as they will be running multiple runs throughout the tournament.

5-8 Person Bracket (run sets of three intervals)

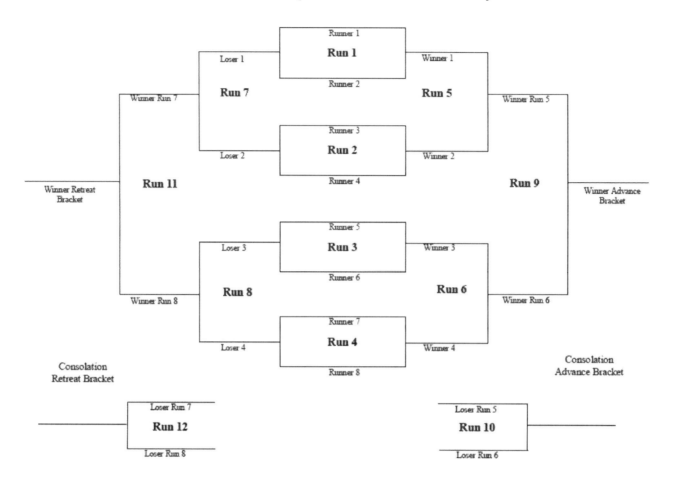

1-4 person bracket (run sets of two intervals)

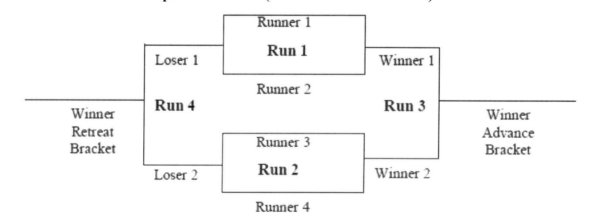

Runner's Pentathlon

Objective: To determine the best all-around runner with a mixture of short and long runs scored decathlon style.

Description: Each runner will compete in five track runs (1500 meters-400 meters-800 meters-200 meters-3000 meters) with 10-30 minutes recovery time between runs. Points are scored for each run based on the running time with the use of a decathlon scoring type chart (see page 142). With an equal mix of sprints and distance events this challenging competition puts sprinters against distance runners to determine the best all-around track runner. Every runner runs the 1500 meters. Their time is recorded on the scoring chart. Compare the time to the corresponding score on the scoring tables and record their score in points. Give the runners a certain amount of recovery time (15 minutes for workout, 20-30 minutes if you are using it as a competition). Start the next event, the 400 meters and time everyone. Record on the scoring chart and record the points off the scoring tables. Keep a running cumulative total. After the last event, complete the event by announcing the point totals.

Variations: Use a short version of the Runner's Pentathlon by using half of the distances. 800-200-400-100-1500. In hot weather, the shorter distance is preferred.

Equipment: Scoring chart, scoring tables, stopwatches

Points	100 meters	200 meters	400 meters	800 meters	1500 meters	3000 meters
1400	9.9	19.78	44.45	1:46.79	3:37.46	7:41.64
1390	9.96	19.9	44.72	1:47.30	3:38.61	7:44.28
1380	10.01	20.02	44.99	1:47.81	3:39.77	7:46.94
1370	10.06	20.14	45.27	1:48.33	3:40.93	7:49.60
1360	10.11	20.26	45.54	1:48.85	3:42.10	7:52.27
1350	10.17	20.38	45.81	1:49.37	3:43.27	7:54.95
1340	10.22	20.5	46.09	1:49.89	3:44.44	7:57.64
1330	10.27	20.62	46.37	1:50.41	3:45.62	8:00.34
1320	10.33	20.74	46.64	1:50.94	3:46.81	8:03.05
1310	10.38	20.86	46.92	1:51.47	3:48.00	8:05.77
1300	10.43	20.99	47.2	1:52.00	3:49.19	8:08.50
1290	10.49	21.11	47.48	1:52.53	3:50.39	8:11.24
1280	10.54	21.23	47.76	1:53.06	3:51.59	8:14.00
1270	10.6	21.36	48.05	1:53.60	3:52.80	8:16.76
1260	10.65	21.48	48.33	1:54.14	3:54.01	8:19.53
1250	10.71	21.61	48.62	1:54.68	3:55.22	8:22.32
1240	10.76	21.73	48.9	1:55.22	3:56.45	8:25.11
1230	10.82	21.86	49.19	1:55.76	3:57.67	8:27.92
1220	10.87	21.99	49.48	1:56.31	3:58.90	8:30.74
1210	10.93	22.12	49.77	1:56.86	4:00.14	8:33.57
1200	10.99	22.24	50.06	1:57.41	4:01.38	8:36.41
1190	11.04	22.37	50.35	1:57.96	4:02.63	8:39.27
1180	11.1	22.5	50.64	1:58.52	4:03.88	8:42.13
1170	11.16	22.63	50.94	1:59.08	4:05.14	8:45.01
1160	11.21	22.76	51.23	1:59.64	4:06.40	8:47.90
1150	11.27	22.89	51.53	2:00.20	4:07.67	8:50.81
1140	11.33	23.02	51.83	2:00.77	4:08.94	8:53.72
1130	11.39	23.15	52.03	2:01.34	4:10.22	8:56.63
1120	11.44	23.29	52.43	2:01.91	4:11.51	8:59.59
1110	11.5	23.42	52.73	2:02.48	4:12.80	9:02.55
1100	11.56	23.55	53.04	2:03.06	4:14.09	9:05.52
1090	11.62	23.69	53.34	2:03.63	4:15.40	9:08.52
1080	11.68	23.82	53.65	2:04.22	4:16.71	9:11.49
1070	11.74	23.96	53.95	2:04.80	4:18.02	9:14.50
1060	11.8	24.09	54.26	2:05.39	4:19.34	9:17.53
1050	11.86	24.23	54.57	2:05.97	4:20.67	9:20.56
1040	11.92	24.37	54.89	2:06.57	4:22.00	9:23.62
1030	11.98	24.5	55.2	2:07.16	4:23.34	9:26.68
1020	12.04	24.64	55.52	2:07.76	4:24.69	9:29.76
1010	12.1	24.78	55.83	2:08.36	4:26.04	9:32.86
1000	12.16	24.92	56.15	2:08.96	4:27.40	9:35.97
990	12.23	25.06	56.47	2:09.57	4:28.77	9:39.10
980	12.29	25.2	56.79	2:10.18	4:30.14	9:42.25
970	12.35	25.35	57.12	2:10.79	4:31.52	9:45.41
960	12.41	25.49	57.44	2:11.41	4:32.91	9:48.58
950	12.48	25.63	57.77	2:12.03	4:34.30	9:51.77
940	12.54	25.78	58.1	2:12.65	4:35.70	9:54.98
930	12.6	25.92	58.43	2:13.28	4:37.11	9:58.21
920	12.67	26.07	58.76	2:13.91	4:38.53	10:01.46

Points	100 meters	200 meters	400 meters	800 meters	1500 meters	3000 meters
910	12.73	26.22	59.09	2:14.54	4:39.96	10:04.72
900	12.8	26.36	59.43	2:15.17	4:41.39	10:08.00
890	12.86	26.51	59.77	2:15.81	4:42.83	10:11.30
880	12.93	26.66	1:00.10	2:16.64	4:44.28	10:14.61
870	12.99	26.81	1:00.45	2:17.10	4:45.74	10:17.95
860	13.06	26.96	1:00.79	2:17.76	4:47.20	10:21.30
850	13.13	27.11	1:01.13	2:18.41	4:48.68	10:24.68
840	13.19	27.27	1:01.48	2:19.07	4:50.16	10:28.07
830	13.26	27.42	1:01.83	2:19.73	4:51.65	10:31.49
820	13.33	27.57	1:02.18	2:20.40	4:53.15	10:34.92
810	13.4	27.73	1:02.54	2:21.07	4:54.66	10:38.38
800	13.47	27.89	1:02.89	2:21:74	4:56.18	10:41.85
790	13.54	28.04	1:03.25	2:22.42	4:57.71	10:45.35
780	13.61	28.2	1:03.61	2:23.10	4:59.25	10:48.88
770	13.68	28.36	1:03.97	2:23.79	5:00.79	10:52.42
760	13.75	28.52	1:04.34	2:24.48	5:02.35	10:55.99
750	13.82	28.68	1:04.71	2:25.18	5:03.92	10:59.58
740	13.89	28.85	1:05.08	2:25.88	5:05.50	11:03.19
730	13.96	29.01	1:05.45	2:26.59	5:07.09	11:06.83
720	14.03	29.18	1:05.82	2:27.30	5:08.69	11:10.50
710	14.11	29.34	1:06.20	2:28.01	5:10.30	11:14.19
700	14.18	29.51	1:06.58	2:28.73	5:11.93	11:17.90
690	14.25	29.68	1:06.96	2:29.46	5:13.56	11:21.65
680	14.33	29.85	1:07.35	2:30.19	5:15.21	11:25.42
670	14.4	30.02	1:07.74	2:30.93	5:16.87	11:29.21
660	14.48	30.19	1:08.13	2:31.67	5:18.54	11:33.04
650	14.55	30.36	1:08.52	2:32.42	5:20.22	11:36.89
640	14.63	30.54	1:08.92	2:33.17	5:21.92	11:40.78
630	14.71	30.71	1:09.32	2:33.93	5:23.63	11:44.69
620	14.79	30.89	1:09.73	2:34.70	5:25.35	11:48.64
610	14.87	31.07	1:10.13	2:35.47	5:27.09	11:52.62
600	14.94	31.25	1:10.54	2:36.25	5:28.84	11:56.63
590	15.02	31.43	1:10.96	2:37.03	5:30.61	12:00.68
580	15.11	31.62	1:11.37	2:37.82	5:32.29	12:04.76
570	15.19	31.8	1:11.80	2:38.62	5:34.19	12:08.87
560	15.27	31.99	1:12.22	2:39.42	5:36.00	12:13.02
550	15.35	32.18	1:12.65	2:40.24	5:37.83	12:17.21
540	15.43	32.37	1:13.08	2:41.06	5:39.68	12:21.44
530	15.52	32.56	1:13.52	2:41.88	5:41.54	12:25.70
520	15.6	32.75	1:13.96	2:42.72	5:43.43	12:30.01
510	15.69	32.95	1:14.40	2:43.56	5:45.32	12:34.36
500	15.78	33.15	1:14.85	2:44.41	5:47.24	12:38.75
490	15.86	33.35	1:15.31	2:45.27	5:49.18	12:43.18
480	15.95	33.55	1:15.76	2:46.16	5:51.14	12:47.66
470	16.04	33.75	1:16.23	2:47.02	5:53.11	12:52.19
460	16.13	33.96	1:16.70	2:47.91	5:55.11	12:56.77
450	16.22	31.17	1:17.17	2:48.81	5:57.13	13:01.39
440	16.32	34.38	1:17.65	2:49.71	5:59.18	13:06.07
430	16.41	34.59	1:18.13	2:50.63	6:01.24	13:10.80

Points	100 meters	200 meters	400 meters	800 meters	1500 meters	3000 meters
420	16.51	34.8	1:18.62	2:51.56	6:03.33	13:15.59
410	16.6	35.02	1:19.12	2:52.50	6:05.45	13:20.43
400	16.7	35.24	1:19.62	2:53.45	6:07.59	13:25.33
390	16.8	35.47	1:20.13	2:54.41	6:09.76	13:30.30
380	16.9	35.69	1:20.64	2:55.39	6:11.96	13:35.32
370	17	35.92	1:21.16	2:56.38	6:14.18	13:40.42
360	17.1	36.15	1:21.69	2:57.38	6:16.44	13:45.58
350	17.2	36.39	1:22.23	2:58.39	6:18.73	13:50.82
340	17.31	36.63	1:22.77	2:59.42	6:21.05	13:56.13
330	17.41	36.87	1:23.32	3:00.47	6:23.40	14:01.52
320	17.52	37.12	1:23.88	3:01.53	6:25.79	14:07.00
310	17.63	37.37	1:24.45	3:02.61	6:28.22	14:12.56
300	17.74	37.62	1:25.03	3:03.71	6:30.69	14:18.21
290	17.86	37.88	1:25.62	3:04.82	6:33.20	14:23.95
280	17.97	38.14	1:26.21	3:05.95	6:35.75	14:29.80
270	18.09	38.41	1:26.82	3:07.11	6:38.35	14:35.75
260	18.21	38.68	1:27.44	3:08.28	6:41.00	14:41.81
250	18.33	39.96	1:28.08	3:09.48	6:43.70	14:47.99
240	18.46	39.25	1:28.72	3:10.70	6:46.45	14:54.29
230	18.58	39.53	1:29.38	3:11.95	6:49.27	15:00.73
220	18.71	39.83	1:30.05	3:13.23	6:52.14	15:07.31
210	18.85	40.13	1:30.74	3:14.53	6:55.08	15:14.04
200	18.98	40.44	1:31.45	3:15.87	6:58.09	15:20.93
190	19.12	40.76	1:32.17	3:17.24	7:01.18	15:27.99
180	19.27	41.09	1:32.91	3:18.65	7:04.35	15:35.25
170	19.41	41.42	1:33.67	3:20.10	7:07.60	15:42.71
160	19.57	41.77	1:34.46	3:21.59	7:10.96	15:50.39
150	19.72	42.13	1:35.27	3:23.12	7:14.42	15:58.32
140	19.88	42.49	1:36.11	3:24.71	7:18.00	16:06.51
130	20.05	42.88	1:36.98	3:26.36	7:21.71	16:15.00
120	20.23	43.27	1:37.88	3:28.07	7:25.57	16:23.83
110	20.41	43.69	1:38.82	3:29.86	7:29.59	16:33.03
100	20.6	44.12	1:39.81	3:31.72	7:33.80	16:42.67
90	20.8	44.58	1:40.85	3:33.69	7:38.22	16:52.79
80	21.01	45.06	1:41.94	3:35.77	7:42.90	17:03.50
70	21.24	45.57	1:43.11	3:37.98	7:47.88	17:14.90
60	21.48	46.12	1:44.36	3:40.35	7:52.23	17:27.15
50	21.74	46.72	1:45.72	3:42.94	7:59.04	17:40.46
40	22.03	47.38	1:47.23	3:45.79	8:05.48	17:55.19
30	22.36	48.14	1:48.94	3:49.04	8:12.78	18:11.92
20	22.76	49.03	1:50.97	3:52.88	8:21.45	18:31.75
10	23.27	50.19	1:53.62	3:57.90	8:32.74	18:57.60
0	24.5	53	2:00.00	4:10.00	9:00.00	20:00.00

Chapter 15 - Relays

In track and field, relay races consist of four legs, each leg run by a different member of a team. The runner finishing one leg is required to pass a baton to the next runner while both are running in a marked exchange zone. At one time relays were run by simply touching the hand of the outgoing runner or with a flag used instead of a baton. The flags; however, were considered cumbersome and were replaced with batons in 1893.

The baton is carried by the runner and must be exchanged in the exchange zone ten meters on each side of the starting line for each leg of the relay. In sprint relays (400 and 800 meters) a 1964 rule change permitted the runner receiving the baton to start their run 10 meters before the exchange zone (acceleration zone), but the baton must be exchanged within the exchange zone itself.

In most relays, team members cover equal distances: 4 x 100-meter, 4 x 400-meter, 4 x 200-meter, 4 x 800-meter, 4 x 1500 (or 1600) meters relays. Occasionally, medley relays are run, where the athletes cover different distances in a prescribed order, as in a sprint medley of 200, 200, 400, 800 meters or a distance medley of 1200, 400, 800, 1600 meters.

The goal is to maintain the speed of the baton at all times, which is accomplished by the incoming runner maintaining speed and the outgoing runner building up speed before receiving the baton. The games presented in this chapter are designed to familiarize and develop athletes with both the non-visual exchange used for the sprint relays and the visual exchange used for the longer races. Timing is critical for successful hand-offs in the sprint relays and the games are designed to help improve acceleration of the outgoing runner and develop the rhythm of a fast exchange. Visual hand-offs are often overlooked but are an important part of improving times. If a one-second improvement can be achieved on each leg with a visual handoff, the relay time is improved by three seconds (one second for each of the three hand-offs). Many of the games in this chapter focus on achieving that improvement. Finally, the best reason for practicing relays is they are a great team-building event and they are FUN!

Exercise Exchange

Objective: To practice the visual relay exchange

Description: Designate a running area. Two athletes will become partners and jog around the area with a passing implement (baton, bean bag, rubber chicken). The front partner stays 10 meters ahead of the rear partner. On command, a visual pass is made. After the partner who has the object has accelerated 10 meters after the exchange, he/she stops and executes a movement with the object (such as ten touch toes, or three toss and catches). After the athlete completes the exercises, he/she begins to jog again with the partner, this time becoming the rear partner. Keep repeating for a designated time or a number of handoffs.

Variations: After every exchange, add a different exercise and the athlete will need to do all of the previous exercises before starting to jog again.

Equipment: Baton or passing implement (bean bag, rubber chicken)

Centipede

Objectives: To practice a visual relay exchange

Description: Create groups of four to twelve runners with roughly equal abilities. Give each group a baton. Each group jogs single file together in a line, pretending to be a centipede. The last runner in line should have the baton, and pass it forward while running. When a runner passes the baton forward, he/she then runs to the front of the line.

Variations: (1) Do not switch positions and hand the baton back to last runner and repeat. (2) For a more playful version, pick a category like colors or animals and have each runner call out something that fits in the category before sprinting to the front of the line. (3) While the baton helps keep the group together, coaches can run with the group to help pace and maintain the line.

Equipment: Baton for each group

The Chase Relay

Objective: To practice a visual relay exchange while chasing another relay team

Description: Review proper visual relay exchange technique with the athletes. Place an emphasis on maintaining the baton speed through the exchange zone. Four teams spread out around a 200-meter oval. The runners will go counter clockwise handing off and receiving a baton using a visual pass exchange. One half of the teams are located on one side of the track and the other half of the teams are on the opposite side of the track. The first runner on each team will have a baton and run his/her leg and hand off the baton to the next runner on the team. After the exchange, each "just arrived" runner stays on that side of the track and waits their turn to run again when the baton comes back around. The goal is for one team to catch up to a team that started on the opposite side of the track. The relay ends when one baton catches up to another team or after a designated time limit.

Variations: Change the running distance

Equipment: Batons

Exchange Slalom

Objective: To practice using a visual relay exchange

Description: Set up a slalom course that includes, curves, zigzags and barriers for runners to go around (not jump over). In groups of four (one in front of each other), the back person starts with a baton. The athletes jog around the course. On a designated sound by the instructor a visual pass is made. Repeat the sequence. When last person in line gets baton, it is placed on the floor. The first person picks it up and the sequence is repeated.

Variations: (1) Play the game like musical chairs, when the music stops, the baton is passed. (2) Vary the slalom course obstacles.

Equipment: Baton, cones

Turn and Pass

Objective: To practice exchanging the baton in a visual or non-visual exchange pass

Description: Set up a 100-meter loop course with a 20-meter exchange zone in the finishing straightaway. Runners will need a partner. The first runner in the group runs around the loop. When the runner approaches the exchange zone, the partner will take a hand-off, working on acceleration before receiving the baton.

Variations: (1) Use a non-visual exchange. (2) Use a visual exchange. (3) Extend the length of the course. (4) Add an exchange zone on the backstretch with athletes running back and forth on the field to each exchange zone after they have handed off.

Equipment: Cones to mark the exchange zone and course

Moving Shuttle Sprint Relay

Objective: To have fun racing different distances

Description: Designate a starting line and a second line at 30 meters, a third line at 40 meters and a fourth line at 50 meters. Form teams of four people each. Every runner on each team will race distances of 30 meters, 40 meters, 50 meters and 60 meters. Two runners line up on the start line and two runners will line up 30 meters away from the start line to run a shuttle relay. On command, the first runner races to the 30-meter line. When the first runner crosses the 30-meter line, the second runner can start. Once all four runners have run, the distance is moved back to the 40-meter mark and the shuttle relay continues. **Note:** The relay does not stop, it is a continuous run. Continue until all runners have completed all the legs.

Variations: (1) Make the distances shorter or longer. (2) Make the teams with more or less numbers. (3) Time individuals at each distance and add up each team member's time

Equipment: Cones

Sprint/Hurdles Shuttle Relay

Objective: To practice exchanging the baton in a non-visual pass in a combined sprint and hurdle relay

Description: Set up a 100-meter loop course with a 20-meter exchange zone in the finishing straightaway. Set up two hurdles on the backstretch. Runners will need a partner. The first runner in the group runs around the loop. When the runner approaches the exchange zone, the partner will take a non-visual hand-off working on gradual acceleration before receiving the baton.

Variations: (1) Add more runners to one team. (2) Compete with other teams. (3) Extend the length of the course.

Equipment: Hurdles, cones to mark the exchange zone and course

Sponge Relay

 Objective: To use the sponge as a baton, running with it over your head to cool off with water

Description: Designate the running oval with a starting line and an exchange zone. Form two or more groups with an equal number in each group. Each group should form a single file line with the runners behind the starting line. The first runner in each group will have a sponge. Place a bucket full of water 20 meters from the starting line. An empty bucket is placed at the halfway point on the backstretch. On the command to begin, the first runner starts and submerges the sponge all the way to the bottom of the water bucket and soaks the sponge. Then, he/she runs to the bucket at the halfway point on the backstretch and squeezes all the water out of the sponge, finishes the loop, and practices a visual exchange handoff with the sponge to the next runner in line. The second runner soaks the sponge in the bucket of water, runs to the halfway point and squeezes out the water in the sponge, into the bucket. The relay continues until a team's bucket is filled to a designated mark.

148

Variations: (1) The runner carries the sponge over the top of their head. (2) Run for a designated time and see which group has the most water.

Equipment: For each group: a sponge, empty bucket and a bucket full of water

Run and Get Back

Objective: To perform strides in a relay with a controlled recovery by jogging back to the start of the leg when done

Description: Run on a track or loop course. Form groups of four runners to run a 4 x 100 relay. The runners should take a position on the track spread out 100 meters apart from each other. The first runner runs 100 meters and passes the baton (using a visual or non-visual exchange) to the second runner who runs it to the third runner who runs it to the fourth runner who runs it to the finish line. After each individual completes his/her leg, the individual turns around and runs in the opposite direction (clockwise) back to the original starting position. The time aspect of the recovery is controlled because the runners must get back to their original position in time for the next baton exchange. This is a continuous relay that can be continued for a designated time or distance.

Variations: (1) Form groups of two runners in each group. The runners take a starting position by standing in the middle of the track on opposite sides of the track. Runner 1 starts the relay and runs 200 meters and then hands off a baton or touches the second runner who takes off running. After completing the first leg, the first runner then cuts across the middle of the infield to get back to the original starting point to take the baton from the second runner. After the second runner completes his/her leg, the second runner cuts across the middle of the infield to get back in time to take the handoff. Continue running and cutting across the infield for a designated time or distance.

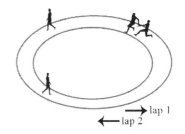

Equipment: A baton for each team

Potato Chip Relay

Objective: To have fun and develop teamwork using a potato chip as the baton

Description: Establish a loop course. Divide into groups with four to six runners in each group. Each group lines up in single file line at the starting line and is given one potato chip. The object of this activity is for the first runners in each group to run to the loop course and return to the start and using a visual handoff, hand the potato chip to the next person to run the course. After everyone on the team has run the course, compare potato chips to see which team has the least damage to their potato chip.

Variations: Run on a loop course

Equipment: Bag of potato chips

Banana Relay

Objective: To have fun and develop teamwork by running with a banana and passing it among teammates

Description: Use a football field if possible. If not, create a field with two goal lines and two end zones. Designate a starting line and a goal line in the end zone. Form groups with six to 10 runners in each group. The runners take their shoes and socks off (a soft running surface is preferred for this activity). Each group lines up with the runners in a single file line behind the first goal line. The first runner will carry a banana. On the command "go", each group runs together to the far end zone and sits down in the end zone, with everyone sitting in a single file line facing the front of the line. The first runner in line puts the banana between his/her bare feet and rolls over on his/her back (backwards) toward the next teammate in line while keeping the banana between the feet. The second runner takes the banana with his/her feet and rolls backwards and passes the banana with the feet to the third runner, who receives it with his/her feet. Continue passing until the banana arrives to the last person in line, where it will be started back up the line. The last person in line passes with his/her feet forward to the next to last person who has rolled backwards to grab the banana with his/her feet. The banana continues back up the line with runners rolling on their back, getting the banana with their feet and passing it to the runner ahead of them. If a runner drops the banana or touches it with any body part other than their feet, the banana must go back to the previous person who started passing it. When the banana reaches the front person, everyone on the team stands up and sprints back in single file line to the starting end zone. The group will pass the goal line and turn around to face the direction it just ran from with the group sitting in a single file line in the end zone. The first person in line holds the banana between his/her feet and the banana is passed from person to person by rolling on their backs and grabbing and passing with bare feet as performed earlier. When the banana gets to the end of the line, it is passed back to the front with the feet only. If a runner drops the banana or touches it with any body part other than feet, the banana must go back to the previous person who started passing it. By this time, the banana will be mush! The front runner has the banana back and is encouraged to peel it and eat it as quickly as possible. The winning group is determined by who can eat the banana and then be the first to whistle out loud.

Variations: Runners leave their shoes on and run to the far end zone. They take their shoes and socks off and pass the banana. They put their shoes back on and run back to the end zone, take their shoes off and pass the banana.

Equipment: One banana for each team, cones to mark starting and turn around line

Note: Pick a person to be the leader of each line that is willing to eat a mushy banana.

Wear the Baton

 Objective: To have fun and develop teamwork while changing clothes instead of handing off the baton

Description: Designate a loop course. Groups should consist of two runners. The group will decide which runner will go first. The first runner will put on an extra T-shirt. On command, the first runner in each group starts running on the loop course or track. At the end of the lap, the runner will take off the extra shirt and give it to his/her partner to put on. Continue the relay using the shirt exchange in lieu of the baton exchange at the end of each lap. Continue for a designated time period or distance.

Variations: The first runner puts on two extra shirts. At the end of the first lap, the first runner takes one shirt off and gives it to the second runner. Runner 1 runs another lap and at the end gives a second shirt to the second runner. Runner 2 then starts running with two extra shirts. Continue to run and repeat the shirt exchange for a designated time.

Equipment: Have runners bring an extra shirt or two, preferably a large or extra-large

Time Zone

Objective: To practice maintaining the speed of the baton while performing a non-visual exchange

Description: Set up a 100-meter loop course with a 20-meter exchange zone in the finishing straightaway. Runners will need a partner. The first runner in the group runs around the loop. When the runner approaches the exchange zone, the partner will take a non-visual hand-off working on acceleration receiving the baton. Coaches will time how long it takes the out-going runner to run the 20 meters from the time they take off until the time they pass the 20- meter end line of the zone. The time is not taken from the hand-off, but from the cone-to-cone distance of 20 meters.

Variations: (1) Use as a visual exchange. (2) Add more runners to one team. (3) Compete with other teams. (4) Extend the length of the course. (5) Add an exchange zone on the backstretch with athletes running back and forth on the field to each exchange zone after they have handed off.

Equipment: Cones to mark the exchange zone and course

Greyhound

 Objective: To work on maintaining baton speed through the non-visual exchange

Description: Form groups of two. Runner 1 lines up at the beginning of the straightaway. Runner 2 lines up at the 50-meter dash mark. Place a cone at the 30-meter mark. Runner 1 begins to sprint as fast as possible. When Runner 1 hits the 30-meter mark, Runner 2 begins to sprint. Runner 1 tries to pass run Runner 2. Both race to the 100-meter mark and the winner gets one point. Both runners walk back for recovery and exchange positions. Continue for a designated number of times.

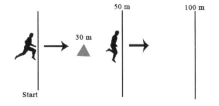

Variations: Runner 1 gets a bonus point if he/she catches Runner 2 and beats them to the 100-meter finish.

Equipment: Cones

References

American Sport Education Program. (2008). *Coaching Youth Track and Field*. Champaign, IL: Human Kinetics.

Anderson, E. & Hibbert, A. (2006). *Training Games Coaching & Racing Creatively,* 4th ed. Mountain View, CA: TAFNews Press.

Athletics Canada. (2006). *Run, Jump, Throw- Teacher Resource.* Winnepeg, MB, Canada: Studio Publications.

Australian Sports Commission. *Athletics Play.* Melbourne, AUS.

Gozzoli, C., Simohamed, J., Malek, E. , B. *IAAF Kid's Athletics- A Team Event for Children.* International Association of Athletics Federation.

Jacoby, E. Fraley, B. (1995). *Complete Book of Jumps.* Champaign, IL: Human Kinetics.

Karp, J. (2010). *101 Developmental Concepts and Workouts for Cross Country Runners.* Monterey, CA: Coaches Choice.

Moving into the Future: National Standards for Physical Education, 2nd Edition. (2004). Reston, VA: NASPE National Association for Sport and Physical Education.

New York Road Runners Club. (2014). *Track and Field Training Program.* http://www.nyrr.org

Pangrazi, R. (2001). *Dynamic Physical Education for Elementary School Children.* Boston, MA: Allyn and Bacon.

Peck, S. (2007). *101 Fun, Creative and Interactive Games for Kids.* Monterey, CA: Healthy Learning.

Quality Coaches, Quality Sports: National Standards for Sport Coaches, 2nd Edition. (2006). Reston, VA: NASPE National Association for Sport and Physical Education.

Stanbrough, M.E. (2014). *Running Games for Track and Field and Cross Country.* Emporia, KS: Roho Publishing.

USATF. (2000). *USA Track and Field Coaching Manual.* Champaign, IL: Human Kinetics.

Weiss, Howie. (2008). *Fun Fitness and Skills, The Powerful Original Games Approach.* Champaign, IL: Human Kinetics.

About the Author

 Dr. Mark Stanbrough is a professor in the Department of Health, Physical Education and Recreation at Emporia State University in Kansas. He teaches graduate and undergraduate exercise physiology and sports psychology classes and is the director of Coaching Education. The Coaching Education program at Emporia State is currently one of only 10 universities in the United States to be accredited by the National Council for the Accreditation of Coaching Education. He was a co-founder of the online physical education graduate program, the first in the United States to go completely online. He received his Ph.D. in exercise physiology from the University of Oregon, and undergraduate and master's degrees from Emporia State in physical education. He has served as department chair and has served on the National Association for Sport and Physical Education National Sport Steering Committee and is a past member of the board of directors for the National Council for the Accreditation of Coaching Education.

Mark has over 30 years of coaching experience at the collegiate, high school, middle school and club level. Coach Stanbrough served eight years as the head men's and women's cross country/track and field coach at Emporia State (1984-1992) with the 1986 women's cross country team finishing second at the NAIA national meet. He has also coached at Emporia High School and Glasco High School in Kansas. He is a Level I and II USATF certified coach. Mark has served as the USATF Missouri Valley Association President and as the head referee at numerous national meets. He is a member of the Emporia State University Athletic Hall of Honor and the Health, Physical Education, Recreation Hall of Honor and has won numerous coach-of-the-year awards at the high school and collegiate levels.

Made in the USA
San Bernardino, CA
21 August 2017